TAKE
RESPONSIBILITY

*How the Best Organizations in the World
Survive in a Down Economy and
Thrive When Times Are Good*

RANDY SPITZER

SelectBooks, Inc.
New York

This edition published by SelectBooks, Inc.
For information address SelectBooks, Inc., New York, New York.

First Edition

ISBN 978-1-59079-204-9

Cataloging-in-Publication Data
Spitzer, Randy, 1952-
  Take responsibility : how the best organizations in the world survive in a down economy and thrive when times are good / Randy Spitzer. -- 1st ed.
      p. cm.
  Includes bibliographical references and index.
  Summary: "Describes how business leaders can create a responsibility culture by changing the social contract between management and employees, encouraging emergent leaders, and delivering customer value"--Provided by publisher.
  ISBN 978-1-59079-204-9 (pbk. : alk. paper)
  1. Leadership. 2. Organizational behavior. 3. Organizational effectiveness. 4. Management--Employee participation. 5. Responsibility.
I. Title.
  HD57.7.S696 2010
  658.4'01--dc22
                          2010002187

Interior book design by Janice Benight

Manufactured in the United States of America
10 9 8 7 6 5 4 3 2 1

Contents

To my son Christof and my daughter Heather
and the millions of middle-managers
and front-line workers all over the world
who count on senior executives to take responsibility
for creating a work environment where people
are allowed to be their best and do their best

Introduction

The best organizations in the world expect their people to take responsibility for their jobs, for continually improving the systems within which they work and, most importantly, for delivering customer value. While the leaders of these organizations have high expectations of their people, they neither bully people into compliance with inflexible policies and procedures, nor do they rely on elaborate bureaucratic red tape to keep their employees and their customers in line. They don't try to manipulate behavior and activity; rather, they give people the freedom to take responsibility for their jobs without supervision. These bold leaders expect workers to measure and monitor their own results, and to be directly accountable to their customers, to their coworkers, and to the organization. Their philosophy about people is: "people really want to be great—and if they're not great, it's because the culture we've created won't let them be great."

Handing over the reins of authority to workers turns out to be a good business strategy. A.D. Amar, management professor at Seton Hall University's Stillman School of Business, and Vlatka Klupic, professor at Westminster Business School in London, worked with Carsten Hentrich, director of IT Architecture at CSC Germany in Frankfurt, to conduct a real-time test of whether tightening control and increasing efficiency at CSC Germany (a $17 billion worldwide IT consulting and services firm) or relaxing controls would work better. They found that when controls were increased, results declined. But when controls were relaxed, that is, when "employees were given the freedom to do things as they saw fit, the outcome was resounding success."

Amar, Hentrich and Klupic discovered that the same thing occurred a decade earlier at telecom-component supplier ANADIGICS during both good and bad economic times. "The $250 million company had found that its centralized, authority-driven structure couldn't respond to the fast-moving industry's challenges and opportunities. They then discovered by giving employees the authority to "respond to changes in the market, so that they could make speedy decisions," ANADIGICS measurably improved their ability to survive and remain competitive. During the good times their revenue increased at a rapid pace, and during a severe economic downturn their people's freedom to innovate positioned them to be even more competitive when the economy eventually turned around. As the three research collaborators discovered, "we've found that contrary to what many CEOs assume, leadership is not really about delegating tasks and monitoring results; it is about imbuing the entire workforce with a sense of responsibility for the business."[1]

Lest you think this philosophy—"people really want to be great"—reflects a certain naiveté about human nature, I concede that we live in a world where people often disappoint us. I acknowledge that ego and the relentless pursuit of self-interest often brings out the worst in us—if we're smarter, more talented, or more powerful than those around us, we may succumb to the temptation of taking advantage of those less gifted or powerful than ourselves. I also recognize that when we feel threatened, we often do whatever it takes to survive, even if it harms us or our organizations. And, I grant that sometimes we are just plain selfish and lazy; it's easier to take care of ourselves and our own needs, rather than worry about taking responsibility for serving the needs of others.

The recent scandal attached to Toyota over their alleged cover-up of sudden acceleration problems in the Camry and Lexus, and braking problems in the Prius hybrid, provides a good example of how companies that I hold up in this book as a model of responsibility can disappoint us. In internal documents company executives noted they had saved $100 million by persuading U.S. regulators at the NHTSA that the sudden acceleration problem was caused by floor mats. Toyota later was forced admit that there were problems with a $15 part manufactured by CTS Corp., an Indiana supplier with whom they had contracted beginning in 2005, during their fast-growth phase. One unnamed Toyota manager quoted in a February 10, 2010 Reuters article said, "The difficulty when a company—any company—becomes big is that employees become detached from the problems. When you can't do anything about this, that's how companies fail. But our job is to drill this sense of crisis into as many employees as possible."[2]

Akio Toyoda, chief executive of Toyota, appeared before a Congressional hearing in February of 2010 to apologize for the need for a recall. In part he said, "Under the banner, 'Let's build better cars' we will go back to the basics of 'customer first' and 'genchi gebutsu' [go and see for yourself], and once more, deeply consider what 'customer first' really means." It seems that Toyota succumbed to the pressures of their enormous growth over the past decade. Whether and how quickly they are able to recover the confidence of the car-buying public will depend upon whether they return to the three strategies that previously made them so successful, which I describe in this book:

In **Part I**, *Take Responsibility for Changing the Social Contract,* I discuss how to change a social contract that inhibits responsibility-taking, and I explain how to build a foundation for a new, healthier social contract based on *Shared Values.*

In **Part II**, *Take Responsibility for Encouraging Emergent Leaders,* I introduce the five things *Emergent Leaders* should be encouraged to do that will help their colleagues take responsibility for taking ownership of their jobs and for finding innovative ways of improving the systems within which they work.

In **Part III**, *Take Responsibility for Delivering Customer Value,* I show how to link responsibility and accountability so that self-managing functional teams and cross-functional teams, called *TransAction Zones,* can consistently deliver customer value.

Other companies I site in this book as models of proficiency have suffered at times as a result of forgetting these three key strategies. Nordstrom lost their way in the late 90s, prompting Bruce Nordstrom to the helm of the organization in 2000 to repair the company's then-flagging reputation. Harley-Davidson has had their problems maintaining good communication with their workers leading to a strike in 2007. Patagonia too admits to mistakes. The point is: no company, even those that I cite as those who "get it" are immune from forgetting what earned them their success in the first place.

Yet, even though individuals and companies behave selfishly at times, I believe human beings also have an enormous capacity to behave with selflessness. Despite the dark side of our human nature, most of us come to eventually realize that life is not simply about achieving our own self-interests, understanding that life is richer by far when we take responsibility for living a life of service to others.

How do courageous leaders take responsibility for choosing selflessness over self-interest? To begin with, these responsible leaders don't waste their time trying to change the behavior of individuals who are unable or unwilling to choose to take responsibility. Instead, these heroic leaders establish a healthy work environment where people from the top to the bottom are motivated to behave responsibly.

Edwin H. Friedman, the man who pioneered the application of family theory to religious, medical, education, business, and governmental institutions, argues that trying to change the behavior of the unmotivated is a waste of time because, as he puts it, "they cannot learn from experience, which is why the unmotivated are invulnerable to insight." No amount of understanding or empathy will cause them to mature or make them responsible, says Friedman. They are the least mature, the most disruptive, and tend to be the chronic trouble makers. They are highly reactive to events and to one another. They place the blame for their own troubles on others—especially management. They see themselves as victims, refusing to take responsibility for their own choices. Friedman summarizes: "there are forces on this planet that, because of their inability or unwillingness to self-regulate, are by nature all take and no give."[3]

Therefore, the wise leader focuses his or her energy and attention on the people who can and will take responsibility. Once a "Responsibility Culture" is established, most of the unwilling choose to leave; and those who don't are eventually asked to leave. Certainly, responsibility-resistant people are given the chance to adjust their behaviors and attitudes (as I describe in Part I of this book) to choose to become responsible. But in the end, people must choose for themselves.

In today's fast-paced, highly competitive world, is it possible to get people to take responsibility when number of the number of organizations and individuals who are avoiding responsibility seems to be growing? The evidence I will present in this book shows that the answer is a resounding YES! As I will illustrate, organizations where people are encouraged to manage themselves and to take responsibility for their own jobs and for the systems within which they work and for staying focused on delivering customer value significantly outperform the conventional cultures where bosses impose control.

When the bald eagle population was threatened, America took action to improve the environment so that their numbers could recover and they could once again thrive—and we've succeeded. So too, organizations that want to survive and succeed in a challenging world must create a *Responsibility Culture* where Emergent Leaders take responsibility for delivering customer value is commonplace; an environment where every member of the organization is free to soar like an eagle.

Part I

TAKE RESPONSIBILITY
FOR CHANGING THE SOCIAL CONTRACT

The summer after my freshman year in college, I got a job as a "helper" for a contractor building a housing development. As a kid growing up I had tried my hand at simple projects like building a table out of scraps of plywood, and as I grew older my friends and I built a tree house in the nearby woods. But at age nineteen on the first day on the job, I had to leave my shiny new framing hammer in my tool belt. When I arrived at the job site the first morning the foreman handed me a shovel and told me to dig a thirty-foot long, two-foot deep trench in the rock-hard clay soil. Little did I know that digging the trench was a test to see if the "new kid" was tough enough to work alongside seasoned construction workers. Six hours later, and despite blisters on the palms of both of my hands, I was still digging when the boss came by to check on the construction crew's progress. He walked up to where I was sweating away and watched me dig for thirty seconds or so. He reached around to his back pocket and pulled out a pair of leather work gloves, tossed them to me and said, "You might want to wear these, kid." Then, he turned and walked up a pile of dirt and slipped between two studs on the outer wall and began an animated conversation with the foreman.

The next day I arrived at the worksite early, put on the leather gloves over my bandaged hands, and started in again on digging the trench. When the foreman arrived, he looked over at me, gathered his tools and began walking toward the house. "Follow me," he said tersely, "I've got something else for you to do today." Dropping my shovel, I followed the foreman up onto the plywood subflooring of the house. "The boss expects me to get the ceiling joists into place before the pre-fab rafters are delivered tomorrow; and since he sent the rest of the crew to help finish up at another job site today, you and me are gonna get this done. I'm sticking my neck out by having you help with this, so you better not foul it up … rookie."

So began my initiation into the world of construction. Being the rookie on the crew, I was treated like a slave. I was regularly sworn at, threatened, blamed for screw-ups, and otherwise verbally abused on a daily basis. So I learned to keep my mouth shut and do what I was told. While I was not the only man on the job who was the object of the foreman's daily abuse, I noticed that the more experienced members of the crew had other ways of coping. For one thing, I observed that when the foreman wasn't watching, some of the crew would deliberately slow down their pace of work, quickly picking it up again whenever he was within sight. Over coffee breaks they'd complain endlessly about the boss. It wasn't unusual for one of the crew to just quit showing up for work without warning. One morning the crew arrived to find the job site had been vandalized. Later that day, I overheard one of the workers whispering to a buddy that he'd done it as payback for having his hours cut.

Perhaps your early work experiences weren't as bad as mine. Yet too often, people find themselves working for bosses who act like bullies, and with coworkers who are discouraged, unmotivated, or even destructive. Oddly enough, it turns out that these behaviors are not usually a result of having hired the wrong people (which, of course, is always a possibility). Instead they are a predictable result of normal human beings trapped in a toxic work environment. Put simply, toxic organizational cultures bring out the worst in people. The first step toward addressing this common situation is to take responsibility for challenging the current social contract.

Challenging the Social Contract

Thomas Hobbes, the first modern philosopher to articulate a detailed social contract theory, contended that people allow others to rule over them in return for their protection. This is the social contract that most workers enter into when they accept a job: they agree to do what those in authority tell them to do in exchange for their wages and some measure of job security. Every group of people who live and/or work together learn to get along by observing the often unwritten, and commonly understood, social contract. A social contract tells people what to expect of one another, what roles they play, and how to be successful in the group. Elementary school kids observe a social contract that tells them where they fit in on the playground. The strong and the swift kids rule over the weak and the slow. In a college fraternity the upperclassmen rule over the pledges. Those who rule either by intimidation or subtle manipulation fight hard to preserve the status quo.

To those in positions of authority, telling others what to do and how to do it may seem perfectly appropriate—especially if those under their authority seem to be unable or unwilling to take responsibility. But why is it that people who are able to function as responsible adults off the job, such as by raising a family, participating in community-building activities, and paying their taxes, fail to behave responsibly on the job? I would submit that this occurs because these people are simply conforming to a social contract that really doesn't expect them to behave responsibly. What's even more unfortunate is that when people in a conventional work environment are finally given a small amount of authority, they often show symptoms of what I call "The Deputy Fife Syndrome."

The Deputy Fife Syndrome

What is the Deputy Fife Syndrome? The syndrome describes symptoms and behaviors of those who assert control or authority in an inappropriate or destructive manner—as a bully. If you have ever watched "classic television" you know that Barney Fife was the hyperkinetic and comically inept deputy sheriff played by the late Don Knotts on the 1960s television series, *The Andy Griffith Show*. It was Barney's ham-handed approach to exercising his power and authority as a deputy sheriff that often got him into trouble. Undoubtedly, you've seen people in the workplace who behave like Deputy Fife: the coworker who, when put in charge of a meeting, shuts down any ideas other than his own by banging his fist like a judge pounding a gavel; the newly-promoted frontline supervisor who issues orders to his former coworkers like a drill sergeant; the middle-manager who micro-manages everything, insisting that every action and expenditure be approved by him; the senior executive who issues draconian rules in response to every little mistake.

> **The Deputy Fife Syndrome is a pattern of behavior of asserting control or authority in an inappropriate or destructive manner—as a bully.**

As a customer, you've also no doubt experienced people who display symptoms of the Deputy Fife Syndrome: the technical support person who refuses to help you resolve a software problem in simple language you can understand; the retail clerk who takes an officious tone while explaining that you can't return a pair of pants without a receipt—even though he has access to a computer record of your purchase; the maitre d' at a restaurant who refuses to seat you ten minutes before your reservation even though the table is open and waiting; the traffic cop who treats you like one of the FBI's ten-most-wanted criminals even though he pulled you over because your left brake light was out. The justification often given by these bullies is that they are "just following the rules" (of the social contract).

Don't misunderstand this. The rules of the social contract are useful in that they give us the boundaries within which we can be successful. Rules keep us from harm. Rules provide structure upon which society or an organization can function and thrive. While rules help us get along with our neighbors and resolve our disputes, the rules can also get in the way, and in the hands of someone behaving like Deputy Fife, can be used as weapons. Deputy Fife's problem was that he enforced the rules at the wrong times and for the wrong reasons. Rules were a vehicle for asserting his limited authority over others, and in so doing, protecting his fragile self-esteem.

For someone susceptible to the Deputy Fife Syndrome, being given a small amount of power and authority can be like taking a powerful drug. Having felt powerless in the past or having been victimized by their abusive bosses, the Deputy Fifes of the world are likely to exercise their new-found authority with great zeal, but often without compassion or wisdom. When given the opportunity to exercise even a small measure of authority, a worker who has been abused by other Deputy Fifes may become a bully.

Managers and supervisors showing symptoms of The Deputy Fife Syndrome may justify their bullying behavior by rationalizing that the people working for them can't be trusted. They base this on their experience that the more they assert their authority, the more the people who report to them resist and disappoint them. Like Deputy Fife, they may see themselves as morally superior. They never stop to think that their authoritarian application of power might be the cause of responsibility-inhibiting behaviors and poor performance. They prefer to believe that lazy, incompetent, and morally deficient people surround them. When the pressure is really on, Deputy Fifes have a tendency to try to bring order out of chaos by bullying the people under them into compliance.

One of the underlying reasons people put in to a position of authority behave like bullies is what Dr. Carol Dweck calls a "fixed mindset." "The fixed mindset creates an urgency to prove yourself over and over," says Dr. Dweck. "If you have only a certain amount of intelligence, a certain personality, and a certain moral character—well, then, you'd better prove that you have a healthy dose of them."[4]

In other words, people with a fixed mindset tend to believe that their talents and abilities are set in stone, so they try to look smart and talented at all costs. They avoid anything that might make them look stupid or incompetent and employ tactics to shift the blame for their failures onto others. What often looks like a display of excessive pride and arrogance often turns out to be a cover for underlying insecurity, low self-esteem, or even self-loathing.

Toxic Social Contracts

A more disturbing reason that people in positions of authority tend to bully others was brought out in the famous *Stanford Prison Experiment* in which Philip Zimbardo and his colleagues at Stanford University divided a small group of college-student volunteers into inmates and guards and placed them into a simulated prison environment. The results of the experiment showed how quickly a toxic social contract can bring out the dark side of our human nature and cause people to behave in ways that are destructive. The experiment, originally designed to go on for a full week spiraled out of control in just four days. The guard's treatment of the prisoners had pushed a few of the prisoners to the brink of psychological break-down.

Zimbardo summed up the bullying behavior observed in the young men assigned to the role of guards this way: "ordinary, normal, healthy young men succumbed to, or were seduced by, the social forces inherent in that behavioral context [having absolute power and control over the prisoners] ... The line between good and evil, once thought to be impermeable, proved instead to be quite permeable." In short, the behavior of the young men who were assigned as guards very quickly became brutal.

The social dynamics that turn good people into bullies is quite complex. Beside the factors already mentioned, they include the need to belong, the tendency for excessive conformity and compliance, a desire to be part of the "in group," and hostility toward the "out group." These common human needs "can be perverted into an excessive exercise of power to dominate others [by those placed in positions of authority] or learned helplessness [for those in positions of subservience]."[5]

The young men cast in the role of prisoners in the Stanford Prison Experiment quickly showed evidence of "learned helplessness" as they were subjected to the dehumanizing effects of the guard's brutal tactics. In order to survive in a very hostile environment these young men cast in the role of prisoners suppressed their normal emotions, identity, and moral compass. Instead, they did whatever they felt they had to do in order to survive.

For many people in America and throughout the world, the social contract has created a work environment that is like a prison. Like the Stanford Prison Experiment, people in conventional top-down cultures are divided into two groups: managers (guards) and workers (prisoners) with very similar toxic behavioral results. The managers often become bullies—even if they don't behave that way elsewhere—and the workers become "difficult," often resorting to an array of responsibility-avoiding behaviors. Both the managers and the workers are doing their best to adapt and survive in a toxic social contract. It's not that these conventional organizations have somehow recruited and hired "bullies" as managers and "helpless" or "difficult" workers. To the contrary, most of these organizations recruit normal, hard-working, well-intentioned human beings. But very quickly, a toxic social contract brings out the worst in people.

You've read the headlines: **Fund Manager Bilks Investors Out of Billions of Dollars; CEO of Major Company Convicted of Fraud; Government Official Found Guilty of Graft and Corruption.** How do these things happen? Are these "white-collar criminals" somehow different from the rest of us? Are they simply sociopaths who eventually are found out because they let their greed overcome their efforts to keep their crimes hidden? Perhaps. However, these lawbreakers are seldom able to commit these crimes without the collusion of coworkers who remain silent. Their coworkers know, or at least suspect that something wrong is going on, yet choose not to confront the wrong-doing because they fear they might be either implicated or fired. They have good reason to have fear. Our society's whistle-blowers have often suffered greatly for having done the right thing.

Very slowly, by simply choosing to ignore wrong-doing, a new social contract evolves: one in which toxic behaviors become the group norm. Seeing that those in authority either ignore or condone toxic behavior, others either join in or simply look the other way. While some members of the group might be bothered by what's going on, they are afraid to confront it. Unfortunately, this state of affairs is something like boiling a frog. If you place a live frog in a pot of tepid water and slowly increase the temperature of the water, the frog doesn't notice the increasing temperature until it's too late. In much the same way, people living under a social contract where toxic behavior is tolerated or ignored often find themselves in the pot with the other frogs.

On the other hand, Cultures of Responsibility encourage people to challenge any behavior that threatens the health of the organization. They establish a high standard of honesty and integrity, which they protect vigorously; they encourage an open-mindset, and have broken down the walls between management and labor by establishing a new social contract based on *Shared Values*.

ONE
ESTABLISH A NEW SOCIAL CONTRACT

Build a Foundation on Shared Values

In 1972 graduate students in the sociology department of a major university in the United States began a research project seeking a link between individual job satisfaction and an organizational success. Initially they surveyed nearly two-and-a-half million workers and managers in the United States across thirty-two different industries. No conclusive correlations or links were found. These graduate students then broadened their research to forty countries. This expansion generated an additional fourteen-and-a-half million survey responses, for a total of seventeen million survey responses. Unfortunately for them, after almost three years of work they found no conclusive statistical correlation between individual job satisfaction and organizational performance. Reluctantly, the graduate students and their faculty advisors abandoned their work, concluding that the data was of little or no value.

The survey data gathered dust in a dark corner of the university's dead files until fifteen years later when through a chance encounter Lebow Company, Inc. (LCI) became aware of the data, was given access to the computer records and started their own investigation. LCI used a methodology John Naisbitt, former Assistant Secretary of Education to President Kennedy had employed to write his bestseller, *MegaTrends*. By measuring and recording the total column inches in newspapers and magazines devoted to news stories, Naisbitt was able to predict with uncanny accuracy future social, political, spiritual and economic megatrends.

Using the same methodology, LCI looked for the words and phrases that occurred most often in the *comments* section at the end of the survey. With the aid of a computer-aided word-search program, LCI was able to identify eight recurring themes which they later called *Shared Values*. These eight shared values seemed to be universal, common to people all over the world regardless of nationality, race, religion, gender, industry, social status, or education. Listed below are the eight shared values the respondents said they prized most:

- to be able to tell the *truth* without fear, and to be told the truth
- to be able to *trust* their managers and coworkers, and to feel trusted
- to give and receive *mentoring* without people becoming defensive
- to see managers and coworkers as *receptive to new ideas*
- to feel safe taking *a personal risk* for the organization's sake
- to be given credit and to *give credit when it is due*
- to be confident that managers and coworkers are *honest and ethical*
- to know that *selfless behavior* is celebrated and rewarded

Truth

Sharing the truth, especially when the news is bad, is not easy. Some people tend to "sugar coat" the truth—hoping bad news will go down easier. Others tend to "embellish" the truth—trying to avoid their own blameworthiness for bad news by exaggerating the culpability of others. A more productive approach to truth-telling is to tell the uncompromising truth without embellishment or trying to make the truth less unpleasant.

Share the truth within twenty-four hours. Hoping it will go away if you ignore it, or that you can avoid blame by keeping your mouth shut is not an effective strategy. The truth nearly always comes to light, and when it becomes clear to those who have been kept in the dark that you failed to tell the truth, they feel betrayed. It is far better to share bad news in a timely manner—as a general guide, within twenty-four hours. Obviously, there are times when any delay, even a few minutes, is inappropriate; and there are times, when allowing a couple of days to pass might make sense. A good rule of thumb is to ask yourself: "How soon would *I* want to hear the truth?"

Before delivering the truth, ask the person with whom you need to talk, "Is this a good time to talk?" Using a phrase like this shows respect for the time and priorities of the other person. Perhaps the person you need to talk with is up against a deadline or engaged in an activity that is a higher priority than talking with you at precisely that moment. Perhaps the other person is already aware of the truth you are about to share and is too upset to discuss it with you until he or she has had an opportunity to cool off. Adopting the phrase "Is this a good time to talk?" becomes code to everyone in the organization that you have something important to discuss, something that really can't wait. Using the phrase signals to the other person that you need their undivided attention and that finding an appropriate place to discuss the matter is important.

Approach the other person in a non-threatening way. In other words, be sure that your approach does not put the other person on the defensive. Of course, being aware of factors that may put the other person on the defensive is important. This might include aggressive body language or tone of voice; being in a position of authority within the organization might also be threatening. Your physical size or gender may be threatening. Even the location you choose for sharing your truth can be important. Bringing someone into your office or invading their workspace can be threatening; choosing a neutral space may be less threatening. Think as well about whether you may keep the other person from becoming defensive by delivering the news privately or in a group setting. Depending on the circumstances, one choice is most often better than the other.

Despite your best efforts to be non-threatening, some people, when hearing bad news, will become defensive anyway. In these circumstances, it is very important to make it clear that your intention is to discuss the issue, not to place blame. Do this by being very straightforward about the issue. Make sure your language is simple, understandable and non-personal; and be sure to steer clear of becoming defensive yourself. Avoid sharing the truth in such a way that it is heard by the other person as a complaint or a demand. Rather, after you've brought the issue forward, make a request of the other person. Ask for their help in choosing an appropriate course of action.

Trust

Building and sustaining trust requires effective two-way communication, among the members of the management team, between managers and workers, and among colleagues. Lavishing trust means that people through-out the organization at every level are trusted to take on new responsibilities and to complete projects without needing to be supervised. Trust is supported by three pillars: competency, communication, and character.

The first pillar—*competency*—is the expectation that you understand how to do the tasks necessary to get the job done. While you may lack experience, you at least need enough basic knowledge to perform the tasks without someone checking up on you. Don't let the person who is trusting you to do the job abandon you. Ask that person to make himself or herself available to help whenever you ask for help.

The second pillar of trust—*communication*—is the expectation that you will communicate with the person who has trusted you both while you are working on the project, and at its completion. Memos, emails, voice messages, and reports are inadequate; two-way, face-to-face interaction is the most effective. Earning someone's trust requires that you clearly understand their expectations. Restate his or her expectations in your own words so that he or she has an opportunity to clarify if necessary. Once you're confident that you clearly understand their expectations, ask that you be given the freedom to find your own way to complete the work even when you appear to be struggling.

The third pillar of trust—*character*—is the expectation that we possess the character that merits the trust of others, in other words, that we are ethical. Russell Gough, professor of ethics and philosophy at Pepperdine University asserts that character is a *choice*: "Despite the fatalistic 'I can't help it' attitudes so prevalent in our day, the truth is that we do have control over and can overcome our weaknesses of character."[6]

So, in order to become trustworthy, you must be willing to *choose* to be trustworthy, especially if people think you've been untrustworthy in the past.

Earning the trust of others requires that you prove your trustworthiness every day by being responsible and accountable. Before taking on a new task, reach agreement on a completion date or time and what the finished job will look like. Make it clear that you've *willingly* accepted responsibility for the task. Playing the passive-aggressive game of letting someone *assume* you've agreed to take on a task, and then claiming later that you never actually agreed to is a choice that demonstrates a lack of character.

Mentoring

Mentoring relationships are a dynamic way to share knowledge and experience throughout the organization. Max DePree, former CEO of Herman Miller (famous for the *Aeron* Chair) writes: "The best people working for organizations are like volunteers. Since they could probably find good jobs in any number of groups, they choose to work somewhere for reasons less tangible than salary or position. Volunteers do not need contracts—they need covenants. Covenantal relationships enable corporations and institutions to be hospitable to the unusual person and to unusual ideas. Covenantal relationships enable participation to be practiced and inclusive groups to be formed. The differences between covenants and contracts appear in detail in 'Intimacy.'"[7]

Mentoring is a covenantal relationship. So, before offering to be a mentor always ask the other person for his or her permission. This can be accomplished by simply asking: "May I mentor you?" or May I help you?" By simply offering to mentor as a friend, you send the message that you are doing so because you enjoy helping them grow and learn, rather than to gain a political ally or as a disguise for supervision. Mentoring is available all around you: from more experienced and knowledgeable colleagues, and from new colleagues with a fresh perspective. If someone has offered to mentor you, accept their help without becoming defensive; give your express permission to be mentored. Be open to mentoring from anyone, whatever their rank or role in the organization. Often younger or less experienced coworkers may have surprising experience or knowledge we may lack.

Traditionally, a mentor is a senior, more experienced person entering into an extended mentoring relationship with a junior, less experienced protégé. You've probably been in a relationship like this at some point in your life. Either you've been mentored by someone (perhaps a parent, teacher, experienced coworker or boss) who has taken you under his or her wing and taught you a great deal, or you have been a mentor to someone. As helpful as these relationships can be, the mentor-protégé relationship is typically a power-based relationship, in which the protégé is dependent upon or subordinate to the mentor.

A mentoring relationship in a Culture or Responsibility is more of a long-term peer-to-peer relationship in which both the mentor and person seeking mentoring choose each other. In order for a mentoring relationship to be sustained in this way, both persons must benefit. The person seeking a mentor should benefit from becoming better at taking risks, experiencing a sense of progress, gaining confidence, developing a sense of purpose, and learning to become self-directed. Likewise, the mentor should benefit from sharpening mentoring skills, gaining a skilled and confident partner and, above all, experiencing the joy of watching the person he or she is mentoring learn and grow.

Receptivity

New ideas are the key to continuous improvement and innovation. New ideas allow organizations to remove roadblocks, improve processes and delight customers. Yet many organizations seem to purposely create roadblocks to new ideas. A complicated idea-submission and review-process makes it very difficult for new ideas to be brought forward and adopted. Layers of supervision in a hierarchical organizational structure make getting new ideas to move from the bottom to the top almost impossible. Structures that allow only senior executives to approve new ideas kill most innovative ideas in their infancy. As a result, in most organizations people on the front lines learn to keep their new ideas to themselves or to just stop using their innate intelligence.

Robert Sternberg, professor of psychology and Director of the PACE Center (Psychology of Abilities, Competencies and Expertise) at Tufts University contends that there are really three kinds of intelligence: *analytical* intelligence (the kind we measure with IQ tests), *creative* intelligence (the kind required for innovation) and *practical* intelligence (simple common sense.) "The most successfully intelligent people," says Professor Sternberg, "are not necessarily the ones with the greatest degree of intelligence in any of its three forms. But whether in school or the workplace, they are able to capitalize on their strengths, compensate for their weaknesses, and make the most of their abilities."[8]

Being receptive to new ideas requires an open mind—regardless of the origin of ideas. There are a number of factors that might close your mind to new ideas. You may rationalize, by offering what seem to you apparently reasonable explanations as to why others ideas won't work. You might allow your personal biases, like your dislike or disrespect for certain individuals or groups to close your mind. You may use playing the devil's advocate as a way to subtly communicate to others that you think they are less intelligent than you, and therefore less likely to have good ideas.

To show your receptivity, listen to new ideas with an open mind regardless of who is offering them. Restate the ideas in your own words so that those offering them can clarify. Set aside your personal biases and avoid putting people or their ideas down; rather, ask reality testing questions to help make new ideas more successful. Enthusiastically support new ideas that have been adopted, even when you're unsure of their opportunity for success, doing all that you can to help the new idea succeed.

Personal Risk-Taking

Remaining competitive in tough economic times requires a culture that encourages risk-taking—an environment where people not only step forward with new and innovative ideas, but are courageous enough to act on the strength of their convictions to do what's right. Remaining competitive requires that organizations give their complete and undivided attention to finding innovative ways to keep customers coming back and creative ways to bring in new ones.

Making it safe for individuals and teams to take risks can only happen when you take steps to make it so. It's not enough to simply announce that it's safe to think "out-of-the-box," i.e., to take personal risk for the organization's sake. Organizations must encourage risk-taking by publicly recognizing and rewarding out-of-the-box thinking by visibly supporting this risk-taking behavior. Beyond this, organizations need to take steps to uncover and remove any barriers to risk-taking such as outmoded policies, procedures, processes, and systems that stand in the way of creating customer value. Furthermore, organizations need to encourage everyone in the organization to take the personal risk of challenging any and all barriers to customer value.

The more mature an organization is, the longer it's been in business, the more likely it is that the culture has become risk-averse. Unlike entrepreneurial start-up companies that are typically experimenting and innovating just to survive, mature organizations have likely found some kind of formula that has brought them some measure of success. But as experience has taught us, past success is no guarantee of future success. The trash heap of history is filled with mature organizations that failed to adapt fast

enough to changing market conditions because their cultures stifled entrepreneurial risk-taking. Challenging long-standing policies and processes is
often politically risky. It takes real courage to do this, because in most organizations it is not safe to do so.

Giving Credit

It is so easy to take your coworkers for granted. You depend on them, sometimes without giving a thought to the effort and time they put in on your
behalf. Yet every human being has the need to feel appreciated, to be given
credit when credit is due. Think about a time when you really went the extra
mile for your company or your boss and didn't get so much as a thank you.
Or worse, you developed a new idea or completed a really challenging project only to see someone else take credit for it. How did you feel? Would
you ever put that much time and effort on a project for their benefit
again? Now, think for a moment about a time when some individuals
expressed heartfelt gratitude for your exceptional efforts on their behalf.
How did you feel then? How did it influence your attitude toward them and
the likelihood of putting forth that kind of effort again in the future?

We all want credit when credit is due. But is there a right way to give
credit? Yes, there is. When you give credit to someone, take care that the
praise you give is appropriate, genuine and fair. Appropriate praise is given
in proportion to the contribution, small tokens of praise for small everyday contributions. In most cases a simple "thank you" works just fine. For
larger contributions, appropriate praise is public—either verbally or in
writing. Genuine praise comes from the heart; false praise is given for other
reasons, such as for political gain or manipulation. Also, giving credit to
others should be done fairly regardless of status, or role in the organization. It's very disheartening for an individual who has worked hard and
made a significant contribution to stand by while his or her colleagues or
their boss receives a bonus, a raise, or a promotion.

Honesty

People who are caught committing corporate malfeasance like theft of petty
cash, embezzlement, or fraud often report when they are arrested, "I never
intended to steal from the company." The story they often tell is of facing
some personal financial crisis that required some temporary loan of

company funds that they always intended to pay back. Their coworkers say they're shocked that their friend would do such a thing. They would never admit that they were aware of the theft, or at least suspected that something wrong was going on. Let's be honest. It's tough to confront a coworker you either suspect is involved in dishonesty or you have actually observed doing wrong. It's easier to shake your head and look the other way.

Suppose you see someone walking out the door with a box of office supplies or see them conducting personal business on company time. Should you confront them, or because "it's no big deal," or "everybody's doing it," let it go? The hard truth is that knowing about wrong doing and failing to either confront the offender or report it makes you complicit, whether you choose to become involved in the unethical activity or not. Unethical or dishonest behavior includes more than theft or fraud; simply failing to put in an honest day's work is dishonest too. And yet, disgruntled workers all over the globe engage in a game of "catch me if you can" with their managers—working hard only when directly supervised, and loafing whenever they're not.

Honesty and ethics provides the bedrock of pride in an organization. When people adhere to high standards of corporate ethics that are non-negotiable, when they clearly support their organization's values, when people put in an honest day's work every day, when they take pride in their organization's products and services, and when people are willing to confront dishonest and unethical behavior in all of its forms, a Responsibility Culture becomes possible.

Selflessness

Selfless behavior, that is, putting the interests of others before your own may seem out of place in an organizational setting. But unless your colleagues and your customers feel you are considering their needs, eventually they will stop doing business with you. When asked, "What are the traits of the people you most admire?" people tend put together a list something like this:

■ openness	■ sensitivity	■ caring
■ honesty	■ listening	■ vision
■ trustworthiness	■ truthfulness	■ selflessness
■ courage	■ encouragement	■ knowledge

Did you notice that only the last trait on the list would be considered a technical skill? All of the others describe selfless behavior, behavior that puts the good of others ahead of self-interest.

Family therapist Rosamund Stone-Zander and her husband, the world renowned orchestral conductor Benjamin Zander, write about the importance of creating communities of people who put WE ahead of Us and Them, "More often than not history is a record of conflict between Us and Them. We see this pattern expressed across a broad spectrum: nation to nation, among political parties, between labor and management, and in the most intimate realms of our lives. ... The WE appears when, for the moment, we set aside the story of fear, competition, and struggle, and tell its story. The WE story... points to relationship rather than to individuals, ...[it is] the vital entity of our company, or community, or group of two."[9]

Choosing to be selfless does not oblige you to become a martyr or someone's door mat; rather, it requires that you fully engage yourself in promoting community—in the WE—by helping others succeed, and celebrating their success even when there is no personal benefit for doing so.

Reduce *"Values Tension"*

In 1989 LCI (Lebow Company Inc.) registered the Eight Shared Values™ with the United States Patent Office as a key component of the *Values & Attitude Study*™. LCI concluded that these Eight Shared Values, clearly important to people in all industries and all cultures worldwide, might be linked to organizational success. The Lebow group tested their hypothesis on a small chain of eight family-style restaurants along the I-5 corridor in the western United States. This small study confirmed a direct link between shared values and each restaurant's bottom line. Since then, well over two-thousand-four-hundred operational units* have been studied by LCI and a strong correlation between the Eight Shared Values and operational results has been confirmed. When present, these Eight Shared Values help to create a Responsibility Culture, and enable people perform at their best.

Shared values are the foundation upon which a Responsibility Culture is built. Based on the results of more than twenty years of data gathering with the *Values & Attitude Study*, LCI has validated the correlation between

---

*An *operational unit* can be a small organization or a group/department within a larger organization.

values tension and organizational success by comparing values tension scores against measures of organization success such as profits and productivity. But what is "values tension"? Values tension is the interpersonal conflict that results when there is a gap between what people expect regarding the Eight Shared Values and what they actually observe from their managers and coworkers. In organizations where that Values Tension gap is high, productivity and profits suffer; in organizations where the gap is low, measures of operational success are consistently higher.

It's easy to understand why this correlation exists. Think about it. When you're working in a culture where the level of interpersonal tension is high, a great deal of your energy is expended on avoiding or dealing with conflicts that inevitably erupt. Dealing with constant interpersonal conflict distracts and discourages you from spending your energy on productive activity like completing important projects and tasks, solving problems, and giving your customers your undivided attention. In addition, interpersonal conflict is stressful, and stress negatively impacts both your mental acuity and your physical endurance. In contrast, when the level of interpersonal tension is low, your interactions with coworkers are smoother and easier. You and your coworkers are more energetic and more focused on your customers, on improving your systems, and on solving problems.

Like the results of the original restaurant chain, each organization that completes the *Values & Attitude Study* is encouraged to compare the Values Tension scores of each department, division, or location with their operational results. Over the years we have been able to confirm a high correlation between Values Tension and operational results. Perhaps more interestingly, we have also noticed that Values Tension is also a highly reliable predictor of the organization's success in the following year. A low Values Tension score does not *guarantee* future success because, after all, there are many factors that impact on an organization's success: changing market conditions, changes in customer preferences, and of course the overall economy. In simple terms, organizations with a low values tension score have a much better chance for survival when business conditions are tough simply because their culture is healthier and therefore better able to adapt to challenges.

Increase *Employee Engagement*

When asked, most people in an organization would tell you that they are working hard and fully engaged in their work. However, often what people intend and what they actually do are two different things. While they might intend to behave as good team members or independent-idea generators, others might see them as people who are just going through the motions, or who are angry and frustrated. Can you expect people who appear not to be fully engaged in their work, to become fully engaged? Yes, but you must close the gap between their intended behavior and their actual behavior.

The *Values & Attitude Study* measures this gap by asking people first to describe how they are engaged, and then to describe how engaged their coworkers are. They're given four types of behavior to choose from: (1) a *hero* who is fully engaged with his or her team, (2) a *maverick* who is less engaged with the team, yet is fully engaged in his or her work, (3) a marginally engaged nine-to-fiver who does what is asked each day, or (4) or a mostly disengaged dissident who has become frustrated and angry. In the average organization, about eighty-five percent of employees see themselves as either a hero or a maverick (fully engaged); while on average, only forty-two percent see their coworkers as fully engaged.

This statistic reminds me of the old joke about the woman who has been working at a new job for about a month, when she is asked by her spouse a simple question: "How many people work at your company?" Not knowing the answer, the next day she asks a coworker who had been with the company for a long time the same question. The veteran employee thinks for a moment and then wryly replies, "Oh I don't know, I'd guess about half." It turns out that while most of us see ourselves as fully engaged, we are inclined to see others as less engaged than ourselves. The *Values & Attitude Study* confirms this perceived gap.

The *Values & Attitude Study* shows that healthy organizations have a much narrower perception gap. Why is this? People working in a Responsibility Culture, perhaps because they are given the freedom work in self-managing teams, are much more aware of how engaged their coworkers really are. It's also highly likely that workers in these healthier environments *really are* more engaged in their work.

Tap Into *Intrinsic Motivation*

In the early 1930s, B. F. Skinner, a brilliant professor of psychology at Harvard, developed the theory of motivation he called, "operant conditioning." Based on his experiments where he changed the behavior of rats and pigeons by conditioning them to expect a reward for a desired behavior or a punishment for an undesirable behavior, Skinner concluded that changing human behavior could be similarly accomplished. In his own words: "find the right stimulus and you'll get the desired response."[10] Skinner's theory of human motivation became the justification for industry, government and education to embrace incentives whole-heartedly.

But do incentives really motivate? You bet they do! Incentives appeal to the natural human desire for recognition and money. The problem is that using incentives as the default tool for motivating people to work harder implies that a lack of employee motivation is the main cause of substandard individual performance and engagement. Challenging the assumption that incentives are an effective tool, the conclusions of numerous independent studies over the last several decades have shown that incentives do more harm than good. The researchers found that "incentives do motivate: they motivate people to earn incentives, while often ignoring or overlooking the negative side effects."[11] In fact, people working for incentives report: "they often ignore obvious negative side effects because they consider these issues to be a management problem."[12]

Alfie Kohn, noted author and expert on the toxic side effects of incentives summarizes the argument against using incentives this way: "While manipulating people with incentives seems to work in the short run, it is a strategy that ultimately fails and even does lasting harm."[13] In his powerful book on the subject of how incentives affect human motivation, *Punished by Rewards*, Kohn presents the conclusions of several researchers who have extensively studied the subject. The researchers discovered convincing evidence that Skinner's theory of using incentives to drive human behavior is seriously flawed. While they concede that offering a reward (or punishment) influences human behavior in the short term, they found that motivating long-term behavior is much more complex than Skinner's theory would lead one to believe.

In fact, the study results showed that people being offered an incentive for an activity tend, over time, to lose interest in those activities, even if they previously had enjoyed doing them without the incentive. The study participants became less intrinsically motivated,* that is, less engaged in tasks because they felt manipulated by the incentive. Even more startling, the researchers found that a high percentage of subjects who were offered an incentive either did the minimum required to earn it, or worse, they cheated. In short, incentives tend, in the long-run to discourage workers from staying engaged and excited about their work.

In a brilliant new book, *Drive: The Surprising Truth About What Motivates Us*, author Daniel Pink describes motivation as falling into three categories: Motivation 1.0 is the motivation to meet our basic needs for survival—food, water, air, shelter, and safety. Motivation 2.0 is the use of carrots and sticks to coax people to do unpleasant or repetitive tasks. Motivation 3.0 is intrinsic motivation driven by three things: "(1) autonomy—the ability to be self-directed, (2) mastery—the desire to get better and better at something that matters, and (3) purpose—pursing a cause greater and more enduring than yourself." Pink uses another pair of powerful metaphors to describe motivation: "*Type X Behavior*—behavior fueled more by extrinsic desires than intrinsic ones and concerned less with the inherent satisfaction of an activity and more with the external rewards to which an activity leads," and "*Type I Behavior*—behavior [that] concerns itself less with the external rewards an activity brings and more with the inherent satisfaction of the activity itself."[14]

The *Values & Attitude Study* has confirmed that the most effective motivation for workers isn't the extrinsic incentives of good wages and job security; the most effective workplace motivator is intrinsic—*interesting work*. Of course, the financial rewards need to be adequate to attract and retain the best talent available. But money is not enough to keep talented people motivated. People crave work that is challenging, rewarding and exciting. They need to feel their efforts are significant, and they want an opportunity to really make a difference.

Summary

The Eight Shared Values™ were the key themes identified from studying the literal comments of seventeen million survey responses from people in

---

*Psychologist Harry Harlow first defined "intrinsic motivation" as being motivated by the reward of the activity itself.

forty countries. A positive correlation between values tension and operational results has been validated with the *Values & Attitude Study*. Values tension is a measure of the interpersonal conflict that results when there is a gap between what people expect regarding the Eight Shared Values and what they actually observe from their managers and coworkers. When values tension is high, operational results suffer. When values tension is low, operational results improve. Employee engagement improves when people have the freedom to manage themselves and to work together in self-managing teams. Motivation improves when people have work that is challenging, rewarding, and exciting.

Note

The *Values & Attitude Study* is the most comprehensive measure of workplace wellness available in the world today: With more than fifteen years of data and more than 2,400 operational units surveyed so far, the *Values & Attitude Study* has created a series of workplace culture indexes which, by measuring values tension, motivation, and employee engagement, can accurately predict how well the organization will perform in terms of operational and financial results. For more information visit our website at responsibilitycultures.com or call us at (360)871-7251.

TWO
OVERCOME BULLYING

One of the thorniest challenges facing organizations that are trying to establish a Responsibility Culture is confronting and overcoming behaviors that inhibit responsibility-taking. These behaviors are easy enough to spot in others, especially a boss or coworker. They are tougher to admit about oneself. Despite your best efforts to interact with coworkers as respected peers, you may find yourself caught up in Machiavellian behavior patterns of power and control. According to Niccolo Machiavelli, author of the "The Prince," a good prince may take any action, no matter how cruel or unjust, as long as his action maintains the stability of the principality he rules. It is vital, Machiavelli goes on, that a prince does anything necessary to keep his power, concluding, "It is best to be both feared and loved; however, if one cannot be both it is better to be feared than loved."[15] Unfortunately, "Machiavellian" is a good description of how many people tend to behave when working within toxic environments. To illustrate, let me share a personal story:

> My wife and I were on a shopping trip to the mall when we bumped into the parents of one of my wife's former elementary school students. To keep the story clear, I'll call the parents Mike and Betty and their son David (not their real names.) While Betty filled my wife in on how David was now doing in junior high school, I chatted casually with Mike. Mike had read our book, *Accountability*, a copy of which my wife had given him two years earlier. Mike

said to me, "I really enjoyed reading your book because frankly, before I did, I thought I might be crazy."

Mike explained that he was a mid-level manager at a large government facility near our home. He described how, by using the philosophy we describe in our book, *Accountability,* his department had been doing very well. He had formed a self-managing team giving the members complete freedom to own their jobs without his supervision, to develop their own new ideas, and to find solutions to problems without checking with him. As a result, his people were thriving and his department was delivering excellent results for their customers. At the same time Mike's boss and some of the other mid-level managers who also reported to his boss were operating on the conventional top-down management model. This resulted in a long list of toxic behaviors: political infighting, a growing list of targets imposed from the top, resistance to those targets from those at the bottom, and internal competition for resources. In short, they were not doing nearly so well as Mike's team. What Mike found interesting was that his boss and many of the people in other departments were engaging in a broad range of toxic work-place behaviors. They didn't realize that by adopting Mike's philosophy, his boss and his fellow mid-level managers could soon put an end to those toxic behaviors and vastly improve their operational results.

To be fair to Mike's bosses, even if you intellectually understand the idea of creating a Responsibility Culture by forming Self-Managing Teams and encouraging people to share leadership, it is still very difficult to break free of power-based relationships and patterns of behavior when you've spent years in working in a hierarchical environment. If you're in a position of authority, you might even see yourself as morally superior, while correcting the toxic behavior of your subordinates who seem to lack the moral compass you possess. If you're not in a position of authority, you may see yourself as powerless to change the bullying behaviors of your bosses.

A more effective approach is to learn to recognize and eliminate your own responsibility-inhibiting behaviors. In these next two chapters, I discuss five bullying behaviors and five learned helplessness behaviors that inhibit responsibility-taking.[16]

I give a description of each behavior, and briefly discuss how to recognize and begin to change these behaviors. It's important to note that these behaviors are *coping mechanisms*. They all work at a basic level, usually in the short-term. Otherwise people wouldn't use in them. But in the long term they don't work well, and more importantly, they all damage relationships and inhibit responsibility-taking.

Verbally Attacking

Despite their best intentions, when trying to find a resolution to a particularly tough issue, there are times when people resort to verbally attacking a coworker. Though they intend to stay in control, at some point they become so frustrated with other people's seeming lack of understanding or empathy for their point of view, or frustrated with their inability to get their point across, or just plain impatient with other people, that they resort to personal attacks. People who verbally attack may adopt a harsh tone of voice or even shout. In addition, their body language might become hostile—aggressively pointing a finger, getting into another's personal space or using other forms of physical or psychological intimidation. Their words may become sarcastic or insulting. They may even resort to name-calling, attacking others where they are most vulnerable.

Verbally attacking others is a way to vent one's frustrations. The person being attacked may have no direct connection to the underlying source of the attacker's frustration. Merely because the person is available and vulnerable, he or she may have the misfortune of being the object of attack. Although verbally bullying may make the attacker feel better for the moment and give them a sense of control, this behavior undeniably damages workplace relationships, often permanently.

Delores had worked as a teacher in the public schools for fifteen years before earning her administrator's credentials. Her first administrative job was as vice principal at a middle school. Her primary responsibility was to deal with kids who got into trouble, such as kids who skipped school, got into fights, were caught smoking on campus, and so on. She quickly gained a reputation among the student body as a strict "by-the-book" disciplinarian.

When she was appointed as a principal at one of the district's elementary school a couple of years later, she treated her staff in the same way. When Delores issued an order to the teaching staff at the first teacher's meeting of the year, she made it clear that she expected it to be carried out without discussion. But some members of the teaching staff, who had been accustomed to working in a more collaborative manner with the previous principal, openly challenged her. At first, her barely concealed anger flashed in her eyes. Then when a second teacher spoke up to support her fellow teacher, Delores could hold back no longer, and she lashed out verbally at both of them. After gaining control of herself, she continued with the meeting. However, the tone for the year had been set.

Delores frequently verbally attacked teachers and the non-certified staff throughout the year. The office staff learned to "tip-toe" around her lest they become the object of her verbal attacks. Before the year was out, the teachers had taken a vote of no confidence. With the intervention of the superintendant, things improved slightly and Delores vowed to change her ways. Unfortunately, her reputation had been established and the trust with most of her staff was destroyed.

If, like Delores, you find you have a tendency to verbally attack others, you need to acknowledge the true source of your frustrations—the personal disappointments and slights you feel you've had to endure. You may have grown up in a household or worked for years in an organization where you were the target of verbal attacks. Or, because you are frustrated and disappointed in yourself but lack the courage to confront your own failures, you may transfer those failures onto the people with whom you work closely and see in them your own shortcomings. The obvious antidote is to confront your failures and frustrations and address them, rather than attacking others. When you catch yourself verbally attacking someone, ask yourself "Where is this behavior coming from? What's really going on here? What's really bothering me?"

If you feel that you are being verbally attacked, a good model for addressing this behavior is the three-step *Difficult Conversations Model* [17] developed by the Harvard Negotiation Project. The first step in the model is the "What Happened? Conversation," in which you and the other person each explore your perceptions of what happened, the factors that might have contributed to the situation, and the impact on each of you. The second step is the "Feelings Conversation" in which the goal is to address each of your feelings about what happened without judgments or attributions. The third step is the "Identity Conversation," in which the goal is to understand the self-image issues that are at stake.

When we're verbally battling with someone, we tend to see our own motivations and actions as pure, when in fact, our motivations are often very complex and often times conflicting. The overall goal of this approach is creating a "Learning Conversation," in which the focus moves you away from trying to persuade the other that your version of events is the right one, and moves us toward understanding the other person's point of view and solve the problem together.

Keeping Score

Keeping score is a strategy people use to gain allies with coworkers and bosses. Think about that for a moment. The whole idea of needing to score points to gain allies implies that there is some kind of highly competitive game or war going on within organizations. Too often, there *is* a war going on, a fierce competition that pits peer against peer for prestige, promotions, and pay increases. It is no surprise that this competitive environment and the associated score-keeping, damages workplace relationships by promoting internal rivalries between individuals and groups.

When people find themselves keeping score, it might be because they are working in an environment where no one gets something for nothing. They're likely to hear people saying things like, "I'll do this for you if you'll do that for me," and "You owe me." This "quid-pro-quo" approach of keeping score merely trades accumulated points for special treatment, much like corrupt elected officials trade votes for political favors.

Tony was the consummate corporate scorekeeper who had risen through the ranks partly because of the favors he had done for his bosses and coworkers over the years. Six months ago he had been appointed as the manager of the purchasing department, which served as the central purchasing agent for everything from office supplies to large capital purchases within the company. Now it was time for him to repay his patrons who had helped him secure his promotion.

When Bob, one of his long-time friends and sponsors, came to him asking for help to secure a $150,000 piece of equipment that was not on his current year's budget, Tony went out of his way to help Bob find a vendor with the best price. He even went to the extra effort of putting together a supplemental budget proposal so that Bob could get the item approved by the Senior Vice President of Finance.

In contrast to this, whenever Pete, Tony's long-time rival, tried to get pre-approved items purchased for his department, the impediments were endless. There were always plausible explanations offered for the holdups: mistakes in the paperwork, problems with vendors, a backlog of other requests that were of higher priority over the years. The list of reasons for the delays seemed to go on and on. Of course the real reason Pete had difficulty getting anything through the purchasing process was obvious. It was payback for what Tony considered to be previous slights. In fact, the treatment Tony gave everyone at his rank or below depended almost entirely on whether those people had done favors for him or had hindered him in any way. To his bosses, Tony was always solicitous—making sure that he could do as many favors as possible, in hopes of earning points that he might later redeem. Tony was not alone in this scorekeeping behavior. It had become institutionalized at his company.

Many organizations have also institutionalized internal competition in a variety of ways. Perhaps the most damaging is a performance appraisal system that ranks employees against one another, and awards bonuses, pay increases and promotions based on them. Scorekeeping behavior in the workplace can be greatly reduced by identifying and eliminating all forms of internal competition such as sales contests, incentives and performance ranking systems. Still, even when organizations have taken steps to eliminate internal competition, some individuals will continue to engage in personal scorekeeping. If you find yourself doing this, consider that seeing your coworkers as competitors turns them in to adversaries, perhaps even enemies. Admit that needing to outdo others may be an attempt to cover up your insecurity and bolster your ego.

To stop this toxic behavior completely, you need to get out of denial about your scorekeeping and resolve to partner, rather than compete, with your coworkers. Take steps to build your self-esteem by improving your knowledge and skills. Volunteer to collaborate with coworkers to achieve a common goal rather than competing with them. Give credit to others whenever they make a contribution to the success of the group. Support others who take the personal risk of sharing ideas that may be unpopular and be willing to step up with ideas of your own. Ask for coaching from a coworker whenever you need it, and be willing to coach others whenever they ask for it.

Toxic scorekeeping should not be confused with appropriate forms of measuring progress that don't involve internal competition. People working in healthy organizations measure their progress continually. In fact, as I will discuss later, developing an appropriate group of measures is vital to your organization's success. (Appropriate measures are detailed in Chapter 10.)

Finding Fault

When problems occur, as they often do in every organization, you may notice that some people in your organization have a tendency to look for people to blame. Rather than looking at how the design of the systems might have contributed to problems, these people habitually look for a scapegoat. Looking for a person to blame when it's most often the system that's at fault is a waste of time and energy. According to W. Edwards Deming, considered the father of the quality movement, more than 95% of problems that occur in any system or process are a direct result of the design of the system. So, to reduce or eliminate problems, Deming advised that leaders look for the flaws in the system, not look for fault in the people working within the system.

People who have adopted the habit of finding fault in others might use words like "always" and "never," as in: "You always do that." Or "You never do this." Of course, the truth is that these words are exaggerations and argumentative. Fault-finders may try to sugarcoat their habit by calling it "constructive criticism," offered to help others improve. Don't be fooled by this tactic. Constructive criticism is not often seen as constructive. It's most often perceived as personal and destructive—it strikes at the heart and wounds. A natural defense to criticism is to counterattack, turning the criticism back on the criticizer. This strategy, too, is unproductive, because it merely escalates faultfinding, and does nothing to move the conversation in a productive direction.

Jack was a front-line supervisor in a shipyard. He had been one of a crew of twelve workers whose job it was to retrofit aging naval ships with updated communications systems. Although not a college graduate, Jack possessed the rare combination of gifts of superior analytical intelligence, exceptional practical technical knowledge, and extraordinary creative problem-solving skills. He worked hard and was very good at his job; he was well liked by his coworkers and bosses up the chain of command. So when his supervisor retired, he was promoted to supervisor. Then a disturbing transformation occurred: he constantly found fault in his crew's work.

Retrofitting ships involves removing old and corroded equipment and installing new apparatus in often very tight spaces. Under his old supervisor, and despite encountering numerous unanticipated issues, Jack and the rest of the crew had been very good at staying on schedule and within budget. Under Jack's supervision, things weren't going nearly as well. They were constantly behind schedule and over budget, and as a result, Jack keenly felt the pressure. He became critical and demanding of his crew. He often lost his temper and yelled at them. When asked by his bosses why the work was not done on time, he would blame his crew for their "incompetence." Of course the truth was that Jack didn't have the leadership and organizational skills his old supervisor had possessed. He was a poor coach, he restricted his crew's access to resources, and he took complete control of day-to-day tasks rather than letting individuals own their jobs. In short, Jack was at fault because he had created a toxic work environment.

Finding fault in others when you feel you're not getting the results you want at work is very human. It is hard to break the natural tendency to do the easy thing: to seek out a scapegoat when you aren't getting what you want at work. It's more difficult, but much more productive, to focus your attention on taking ownership for improving your own actions and behaviors, and the system within which you work. A more effective alternative is to reframe your thinking, focusing your attention on the steps you must take to solve problems without assigning blame to others.

Needing to be Right

For those people who have worked or are working in organizations that impose rigid policies and performance standards on employees, "needing to be right" isn't an option. It's an imperative. It springs from a need to be in control. Everything must be done the company way. The only ideas that are valid are management's; the only way to do anything is the boss's way—no matter how well another way might work. If you're in a position of authority, it's your job to decide what to do, when and how to do it, and why it should be done. And above all, if you're in charge, never admit when you're wrong.

People who've taken on the habit of needing to be right might camouflage it by interrupting others so that they are unable to finish explaining their ideas or sulking and playing the martyr when their ideas are challenged. They might try to use guilt to induce others to give in to their "rightness," and in so doing, manipulate others into doing their bidding. They may masquerade as someone who has an elevated level of self-confidence and competence in order to get others to go along with them. All of these behaviors are a smoke screen to allow them to delude themselves into believing they are morally superior to everyone else.

You might ask, isn't being in control, directing activity, and expecting things to be done the "right" way what people in authority are supposed to do? In a conventional management system, the answer is: yes. There is a difference in a Responsibility Culture where the objective is for everyone to own their jobs, own the systems and be accountable for delivering results. Always needing to be right is a toxic behavior.

Larry was the smartest guy in the room, or so he always thought. His displays of ego were legendary. When his work group gathered for their weekly meeting, Larry was the first—and the last—to speak. He didn't share his ideas for others to consider, he presented them as a fait accompli, expecting everyone to agree and go along. It didn't matter whether Larry was formally in charge of a meeting or simply a participant, he would take over the direction of the discussion. When challenged, Larry would, at first, interrupt in an attempt to shut his challenger down; and if that failed he'd take on a wounded expression and question their friendship and loyalty to him. Even when ideas were flowing freely with many contrasting opinions being shared, Larry would forcefully present his opinions, offering not only the reasons his ideas were superior, but also the flaws in all the other ideas. Larry treated the views of competitors (those outside the group) with even more contempt; their ideas weren't just inferior, the authors were morally deficient. He frequently characterized them as "charlatans, frauds and criminals."

Tragically, while Larry really was a smart guy and his ideas were sometimes brilliant, his obsessive need to be right all the time drove a wedge between himself and his coworkers. After a time, many of his colleagues would give up trying to work with Larry and simply transfer to another department or leave the company. To make matters worse, when this occurred, Larry would take their departure as a personal rejection—further proof of their moral deficiency, and justification for further public verbal mockery.

To break this nasty habit, organizations must discard the whole notion of needing rigid policies and performance standards to control the behavior of people working in the system. Instead, they need to cultivate an environment where people are continually experimenting with better ways of doing things. Rather than trying to find that "one right way," a better strategy is to look for ways to continuously improve workflow and remove waste so that the system can deliver more of what customers really want.

If, like Larry, you've acquired the habit of always needing to be right, you must first acknowledge your feelings of self-righteousness and moral superiority. Then, take a healthy dose of humility, and be prepared to admit you're not always right. If you're in a position of authority, create a work culture where experimenting is the norm. Of course, experimentation requires an open mindset in which being wrong is a pathway to learning and finding workable solutions. Moreover, experimentation often leads to important discoveries that could not have occurred any other way. Above all, adopt the attitude that while you should always try to *do* right, you do not always need to *be* right.

Refusing to Forgive

Refusing to forgive is a strategy people use to try to protect themselves from being hurt again. In refusing to forgive, some people construct an emotional wall around themselves which they wear like protective armor. Unfortunately, the resentment and bitterness they feel often becomes so prominent in their outward emotions that it often spills over and poisons their workplace relationships. In effect, refusing to forgive does more damage to themselves and to those closest to them than it does to the person they refuse to forgive.

Here's how this toxic behavior looks: Someone becomes so angry over what they view as the past transgressions of the offender that they explode over the smallest lapse. They might try to control the person who hurt them through shame by constantly reminding that person of their every imperfection, mistake or failure. They may refuse to forgive if the person who hurt them is not sorry enough, has not apologized enough, or has not done enough to make up for past offenses. They may interpret all of the alleged offender's statements and actions in a negative light. And, they may become very self-righteous, seeing themselves as completely blameless.

George and his business partner were working as consultants for a large international company. Several months into the project George and his partner came to a major disagreement over the equitable distribution of the fees they were being paid. Although they tried talking about it, finally out of frustration George's partner (the majority owner of our business) dictated terms—telling George what his share of the fees would be with no further negotiation.

George was stunned and devastated by his partner's refusal to negotiate. So he decided to retaliate by contracting with the international company directly, effectively severing their five-year partnership. Of course, George's partner was shocked and angered by this action, and so he reciprocated by sending George a threatening letter demanding that he comply with the payment arrangement he had previously dictated or face a civil lawsuit. Their friendship and their partnership came to an abrupt end.

For years, George saw himself as blameless and refused to forgive his ex-partner. He was miserable because of it. His emotions sometimes spilled over at the most inappropriate and embarrassing moments. It wasn't until he acknowledged his share of the blame and chose to forgive both himself and his ex-partner, that George found release from the bondage of his own anger and despair. Truthfully, even years later, the pain of what happened remained, but was far less acute. For George and his ex-partner, forgiveness came too late to save their relationship. In choosing to forgive, George empowered himself to create and maintain healthier workplace relationships.

Nations too have chosen forgiveness over retribution. In 1995, when South Africa was emerging from years of civil strife, they established a Truth and Reconciliation Commission (TRC). The commission provided an opportunity for witnesses and victims of abuse to give testimony about the secret and immoral acts committed by the apartheid government, the liberation forces including the African National Congress, and other forces for violence that many say would not have come out into the open otherwise.

The commission was able to bring together those who had been victims of violence between 1960 and 1994 with those who had committed abuses in order to restore the dignity of the victims and to reconcile them with their abusers. As a result, some of the abusers (about one in nine of those who applied) were granted amnesty for their crimes—provided that their crimes were politically motivated, proportionate, and there was full disclosure. Many offenders who were not granted amnesty by the state (and who served prison terms) were nonetheless forgiven by their victims. The TRC is credited with helping to heal the considerable wounds of thirty-five years of strife by providing a mechanism for forgiveness rather than a "victor's justice" in which the victors punish the vanquished with no regard for their own abuses.[18]

Refusing to forgive keeps you locked up emotionally. You become a prisoner to your pain and give the persons who hurt you power to continue to hurt. Although it is certainly not easy and it takes time and persistence, learning to forgive ultimately gives you the strength to break the bonds of your anger and pain. In the end, learning to forgive isn't just something you need to do for the benefit of those who have hurt you and the people closest to you. It's something you need to do for yourself.

Summary

Bullying behavior is any action used to control the behavior of others and to avoid being hurt, such as: verbally attacking, keeping score, finding fault, needing to be right, or refusing to forgive. Bullying behavior inhibits responsibility-taking. These behaviors are coping mechanisms that may work in the short-term, but in the long-term, they don't work well. In the end they damage relationships and inhibit responsibility-taking.

THREE
OVERCOME *LEARNED HELPLESSNESS*

■ **IN THIS CHAPTER:**

Being Passive-Aggressive

Creating Diversions

Playing the Victim

Avoiding

Giving Up

People who find themselves in an untenable situation where they feel helpless to defend themselves often fall into to a state of *learned helplessness*. Philip Zimbardo writes in *The Lucifer Effect*, "Experiencing a loss of personal identity and subjected to arbitrary continual control of their behavior, as well as being deprived of privacy and sleep, generated in them [the young men playing the role of prisoner in the *Stanford Prison Experiment*] a *syndrome of passivity, dependency, and depression* [italics added] that resembled what has been termed 'learned helplessness.'"[19]

Learned helplessness is a coping mechanism often observed in work environments where individuals have concluded that they are powerless to fight "the system" or those in authority over them. Unfortunately learned helplessness is a coping mechanism with a high cost. Not only do people who choose learned helplessness often suffer a loss of personal identity, they also lose any sense of responsibility for their choices and actions.

Being Passive-Aggressive

Passive-aggressive behavior, while passive on the surface, is aggressive behavior none-the-less. When you see a master of passive-aggressive behavior, you see a person highly skilled at subterfuge and sabotage. They're always careful to cover their tracks so that they can maintain a high degree of deniability. Put simply, passive-aggressive behavior is *devious*. In the workplace, you might see people using passive-aggressive behavior to indirectly obstruct those projects and people who oppose them or don't want them to succeed, even finding a way to hasten failure if they can. Catching someone in passive-aggressive behavior can be like trying to prove the existence of UFOs. Although you might have bits of evidence, you can never conclusively prove it. Even though you might have seen them doing something underhanded, proving they intended the devious behavior is often nearly impossible.

If you confront someone about passive-aggressive behavior, they may have some kind of justification at the ready. When working with others on a problem, passive-aggressive individuals may let others make suggestions, but then find an indirect way of tearing the suggestion apart. When others suggest a change or an idea that passive-aggressive persons don't like, they may pretend to be confused. They give the impression that they are willing to go along with the idea, but find a way to later sabotage the idea. If forced to participate in tasks they don't like, passive-aggressive individuals might pretend to be inept so they can manipulate others to step in and do it for them.

Charlie was a bright young man who had breezed through his college business management courses. He was known by his classmates to have a very sarcastic sense of humor. Although he was generally quiet in class, when a practical joke had been pulled, it often later turned out that Charlie was behind it. No one was immune from his practical jokes and sarcastic comments, particularly those who had an inflated image of themselves, or persons who abused their positions of power—including his professors.

After graduating, Charlie got a job as an entry-level manager in a large national company. Because he was smart, at first he rose in the organization quickly. In just fifteen months he was promoted to a position where he had greater responsibility. And, just two years later he was promoted again to a division manager. Everyone in the organization understood these quick promotions meant that Charlie was a rising star with a bright future. Yet within weeks of being assigned his new job as division manager, his prospects seemed to fade.

The same sarcastic wit that had earned him a reputation as a practical joker in college was backfiring in his company's home office culture. Unable, or perhaps more accurately, unwilling to adapt to the political realities, Charlie resorted to classic passive-aggressive behavior. When he was issued a directive that he considered a bad idea by someone up the chain of command, he decided to ignore the directive, pretending he hadn't received the email memo and skipping the meeting where he would have been expected to report his progress. His excuse for missing the meeting was the only one that was accepted in the company culture—a customer was demanding immediate attention.

When he found himself appointed to a task force charged with finding a solution to a production problem, Charlie, who considered himself a "marketing guy," not a "production guy" found reasons to miss most of the task force meetings. When the task force presented its recommendations, Charlie let his friends who were not on the task force know privately in very derisive terms, just how dim-witted he thought their recommendations were. He was always careful to keep a low profile so that he could maintain deniability should his disparagements be attributed to him. As Charlie continued on the path of passive resistance, he began to develop a new reputation: that of being a "non-team player." His career stalled. He was reassigned to a staff position in an outlying district office where senior executives felt he could use his talents and also do little damage.

In organizations where passive-aggressive behavior occurs frequently, it is very likely that it's not safe to directly challenge authority. Passive-aggressive behavior most often occurs in authoritarian cultures where the need to be right is combined with a strong tendency to lay the blame for organizational failures on individuals. In these cultures, employee feedback is often slanted toward the negative (such as focusing performance appraisals on improving weaknesses) and punitive disciplinary tactics are in play (such as suspending workers without pay, and withholding pay increases and promotions.) The obvious resolution to this situation is to move toward a more collegial culture of partnering where levels of mutual trust and respect are high, and where the truth is appreciated, even when the news is bad.

If you catch yourself engaged in passive-aggressive behavior, you need to stop yourself and choose instead to be up-front. Be honest about your thoughts and feelings so that you might convince your coworkers of your point of view. You should also be prepared to support your coworkers with an honest effort to make a project succeed even when you still have reservations about their idea. In short, if you have the habit of using passive-aggressive behavior, you need to stop playing games, and resolve to be more honest and straightforward.

Creating Diversions

Diversions are a strategy people use to try to avoid talking about difficult issues. Using diversions, people hide their real concerns by talking about safe topics, or arguing about one thing when they're really upset about something else. For example, someone might criticize a coworker for being too assertive in a meeting when they're really feeling insecure about their own assertiveness. They might get angry or withdraw if the discussion gets too close to real issues they don't want to discuss. They might talk passionately about resolving "other people's concerns." And then when pressed, they deny that these concerns are their own. When asked directly, "What's bothering you?" they become defensive, or shut down completely.

Because diversions hide one's real agenda, it leaves coworkers confused. Coworkers take the diversions at face value and spend a great deal of energy trying to solve the problems being voiced. Yet because the real issues are never brought forward, they can never be resolved. Diversions are bad for everybody. Coworkers grow more and more frustrated at their inability to adequately resolve the diversions, while the diverters grow increasingly frustrated that their coworkers never figure out what the real issue is, and therefore never resolve it.

Joe was a veteran sales rep with twenty years in the company. He was well liked by his customers. His sales had been above average in the first few years of his career. Then for the last five years or so they had dropped off. Because of his longevity he'd reached the top of his company base pay scale for salesmen; and although he'd applied for sales supervisory positions on several occasions (which paid more), he'd never been chosen. Though the sales team did not have a lot of meetings, when they did call the sales staff together, Joe had become quite the gadfly. He would sit in the back of the meeting room and make a nuisance of himself by starting side conversations, walking in and out of the room during presentations, and more recently bringing up "concerns" during the meeting that were unrelated to the meeting's agenda. Initially, his coworkers went along with his diversions and even joined in at times; and the sales director listened respectfully to his concerns, giving him more "air time" than he wanted to.

Recently, the sales manager announced a major change to the compensation system and invited questions and discussion from the sales team. Joe's diversions became more frequent and disrespectful. His buddies would no longer even sit with him, and the sales manager became more direct, asking him what was really bothering him. Then Joe would divert this by launching into a harangue about how many of the other sales people felt the new system was unfair, but were unwilling to say so during the meetings. The truth was Joe felt he deserved a raise because of his years of loyalty to the company. Joe could see that with the new compensation system he would likely be making less money; and he was upset about it. Rather than being up-front about his concerns, which was way too risky with his fragile ego, he resorted to diversions and drove his boss and his coworkers crazy.

It's tough to talk about your emotional issues, if you have them, when your real fear is that your concerns will be ignored or rejected, or that you will be ostracized. When your coworkers confront you about what's bothering you, rather than resorting to diversions, it's okay to say something like, "I'm not ready to talk about it yet; when I get my thoughts and feelings sorted out I'll come talk to you. But right now I'm asking you to give me some time." Even when you know what's bothering you, it's hard not to get nervous and defensive and to fall back into diversions. It's okay to take the time to sort out your thoughts and feelings so that you can express yourself forthrightly later. Eventually, though, you need to find a safe setting where you can be up-front about your thoughts and feelings and to be honest about what is bothering you.

Playing the Victim

People are most likely to play the victim when they feel they are being treated unfairly. Playing the victim is fueled by a heightened sense of insecurity and vulnerability. When someone chooses the play the victim, they shift responsibility for their problems away from themselves onto someone else. They may look for reassurance from their friends and allies that their difficulties are the result of forces beyond their control. The more effective people are at playing the victim, the more subtly they are able to manipulate their coworkers into accepting their victimhood, and persuading colleagues to take responsibility for resolving their issues and problems, or perhaps even to save them.

Jane was a nurse who had worked for her hospital for fifteen years and had become a master at playing the victim. In team meetings, rather than risk disapproval by saying something her boss or coworkers might not like, she would always remain silent or, when pressed to speak, would express her thoughts as questions. For example, she would say something like, "Do you think this is the right thing to do?" when she really meant, "I think this is the wrong thing to do." Rather than expressing an opposing view openly when it was appropriate, Jane would shut down, becoming sullen and withdrawn. Later, after the meeting, she would complain to her friends.

When tensions erupted between her and a coworker, Jane would always take the blame to try to smooth things over. Yet she was so sensitive to criticism from others that her own friends couldn't tease or joke with her. Jane became so good at playing the victim that soon her teammates would routinely work around Jane, making decisions she was perfectly capable of making herself, and performing tasks that she should have been doing. Even when her friends and coworkers tried to give her a sincere and well-deserved compliment, she would downplay her contribution.

When you play the victim like Jane did, your coworkers become very weary of propping you up. You might think that by being meek and long-suffering, doing your best to get along, you are keeping the peace. Clearly this is not the case. Because of your unquenchable need for reassurance, your coworkers grow weary of your neediness. And for those coworkers patient enough to continue to reassure you, they are in the position of having to give far more to the relationship than they receive. Your boss, too, grows weary of you playing the victim. Because of your unwillingness to step out of your victimhood, your boss is forced to make the choice between working around you and confronting you. Either choice requires extra time and effort.

Breaking free of playing the victim begins when you take responsibility for resolving your own issues and problems. It requires courage to face your personal insecurities and to take ownership for them. Playing the victim is a tough habit to break especially when doing so has, at least to some degree, worked in the past. The most effective way to break the habit is to acknowledge that you've been playing the victim, and give your coworkers permission to "name it" when they catch you doing it. Often, simply being reminded by friends and coworkers who care about you that you're beginning to play the victim again, helps you to stop this behavior.

Avoiding

"If I just ignore it, it will go away." While we laugh when we hear a character on a sit-com repeat these lines, when hearing this at work it's not funny at all, because avoiding problems and sensitive issues at work does not make them go away. In fact, in most cases avoiding them often makes the situation worse. In spite of this, avoidance is a toxic behavior people use with alarming frequency. The syndrome of "avoiding" comes in many forms. People might avoid taking any action that might challenge that status quo of shaky, yet stable workplace relationships. They may avoid talking about the changes they want from a relationship with a coworker because they've decided it's not worth the effort. If challenged by their coworkers about their avoiding behavior, they might say something like, "I don't need to change; you do!"

Sheryl and Pat were part of a twelve-person administrative group working in their company's main office located in a beautiful ski-resort town nestled in the mountains of southern Idaho. The office work was routine, but varied, encompassing everything from answering phones to generating reports. Generally the staff worked well together and got along well, except for Sheryl and Pat. Before Pat was added to the staff, Sheryl had been the unofficial "queen bee" of the office. Although the company CFO, Mr. Edwards, officially managed the office, it was Sheryl who orchestrated the workflow in the office. Sheryl even took charge, without being given the authority, of scheduling vacations. Further, she ingratiated herself to the whole division by rising early each morning and baking breads, rolls, and cookies that she brought into the break room every day. All seemed to be going well for Sheryl … until Pat was hired.

Pat was a degreed and experienced accountant who was hired to manage the office, answering directly to the CFO, Mr. Edwards. She had more than twenty years of experience in administration, the most recent with a Fortune-100 company. Pat had been hired expressly to improve the productivity of the administrative staff, which according to Mr. Edwards, was at about one third of industry standards. In fact, given the company's recent rapid growth, it was critical that the staff significantly improve its productivity.

The first thing Pat did was to take over the vacation schedule, which under Sheryl's control frequently left the office seriously short-staffed.

Pat began implementing a number of other changes, assigning a good deal more work to each staff member. Threatened by Pat's authority and experience, Sheryl tried to rally support from her coworkers to resist Pat's changes. This was difficult since Pat had already inserted herself directly into the day-to-day work of the staff, directing activity and closely monitoring progress so that no one on the staff could avoid taking responsibility. Sheryl did everything she could to avoid contact with Pat; and whenever Pat tried to confront Sheryl about her lack of responsibility, Sheryl would sidestep, saying she didn't know what Pat was talking about.

Gradually the rest of the staff came around, improving their productivity by more than one-hundred-fifty percent and Sheryl found herself isolated. Her closest friends in the office tried talking with her, but Sheryl continued to avoid talking about the situation, taking she did not need to change her behavior. Sheryl's productivity dropped steadily, she took sick time and personal time frequently. Finally, Pat could no longer tolerate Sheryl's behavior in the office, especially her frequent absences and her plummeting productivity. So Sheryl was fired.

Avoiding issues and problems is clearly not an effective workplace behavior. If you have difficulties like Sheryl does, you may find that rather than making your problems go away, avoiding allows your problems to persist or even escalate. To stop this behavior, you need to get out of denial and acknowledge that avoidance damages your workplace relationships. You need to find the courage to confront and talk about your issues and problems, and commit to making the changes in your behavior that will improve your workplace relationships and your ability to be a productive member of the group. In short, you need to stop avoiding and start confronting your issues directly.

Giving Up

Giving up is the strategy of last resort. When people give up, they see themselves as helpless, caught in circumstances that are unchangeable and beyond their control. They see no way out and shut down completely. They give up on relationships with a coworker and just "go through the motions" with them. They no longer protest when that person abuses them. They find it pointless to change because they believe that any change they make will only make things worse. They find covert ways to avoid contact. In effect, they see no alternatives. What's surprising, however, is that people sometimes continue giving up even if the situation has actually improved.

Kevin was the personal assistant to the divisional manager, Max. Max was a hard-charging authoritarian manager, known for producing extraordinary results in record time. Because of his accomplishments, he had risen through the ranks quickly to his senior position before he had reached the age of thirty. Max also had a dark side. He was known to burn through personal assistants faster than a wildfire driven by the infamous southern California Santa Ana winds. Few of his assistants lasted more than ninety days.

Kevin was the most recent of Max's personal assistants. Fresh out of college with a degree in business, Kevin was eager to prove himself. After being hired, Kevin soon became aware of his predecessors' fates and was determined not to let the same fate befall him. But Max was a tyrant. Despite his best efforts, there seemed to be nothing that Kevin could do to please his boss. If Kevin failed to anticipate Max's needs he was publicly chastised. When he was able to correctly guess what Max wanted, Max would change his mind at the last moment and once again attack Kevin for his "ineptitude." Kevin worked like a slave, always at Max's beckon call day or night. Gradually, Kevin's resolve began to fade and after several weeks he finally gave up.

Max's abuse of his assistants (and other members of the staff) didn't go unnoticed by Max's boss, Fred. Fred put his foot down and demanded that Max treat his people more humanely or he would be fired. Surprisingly, Max's behavior began to change. He stopped berating Kevin, and even complimented him once in a while. In spite of this Kevin couldn't see the change in his boss's behavior. Eight weeks had taught him that the only sane course of action was to give up rather than face more abuse. So, after a few more weeks, and despite Max's efforts to salvage the relationship, Kevin quit.

Learning to believe in the possibility of rebuilding a healthy relationship with a coworker after having given up is very difficult, but it's not impossible. It starts when you resolve to hope again. It requires a willingness and desire to rebuild broken workplace relationships by changing your attitude about yourself and about your situation. It demands that you see yourself not as a helpless victim. You need to regard yourself as a self-directed autonomous individual, capable once again of shaping your relationships and your future.

Summary

Learned Helplessness is a syndrome of passivity, dependency, and depression brought on by a loss of personal identity in people subjected to arbitrary and continual control of their behavior. The syndromes of behaviors include being passive-aggressive, creating diversions, playing the victim, patterns of "avoiding," and giving up. Part of creating a healthy workplace environment involves a willingness to confront and change your own learned helplessness. To assess the bullying and learned helplessness behaviors you currently see, complete *The Responsibility-Inhibiting Behaviors Self-Assessment* found on the following pages.

THE RESPONSIBILITY-INHIBITING BEHAVIORS SELF-ASSESSMENT

■ **Bullying Behaviors**

- ✔ Verbally Attacking
- ✔ Keeping Score
- ✔ Finding Fault
- ✔ Needing to be Right
- ✔ Refusing to Forgive

■ **Learned Helplessness Behaviors**

- ✔ Being Passive-Aggressive
- ✔ Creating Diversions
- ✔ Playing the Victim
- ✔ Avoiding
- ✔ Giving Up

The Responsibility-Inhibiting Behavior Self-Assessment is designed to help you identify the frequency of your responsibility-inhibiting behaviors. Some of the behaviors described in each of the behavior categories will not describe your behavior at all, while others may come uncomfortably close to the truth. Don't score the inventory based on how you would like to behave; score yourself based on how you actually behave in the workplace. Be as honest with yourself as you can.

I encourage you to make copies of this instrument and ask one or more of your colleagues to assess your workplace behaviors as well. Discuss whether your work environment is the cause of any of these responsibility-inhibiting behaviors, and what you each might do to help create a healthier workplace environment. Choose to work on reducing or eliminating one or more of your responsibility-inhibiting behaviors.

Identifying the Frequency of Your Responsibility-Inhibiting Behaviors

Instructions: Read each behavior description. Then assign a score indicating how frequently you use this behavior in the workplace. Use the following scale:

---

0 = Never   1 = Seldom   2 = Sometimes   3 = Often   4 = Always

---

EXAMPLE

0	1	2	3	4	0 = Never 1 = Seldom 2 = Sometimes 3 = Often 4 = Always
X					I mentally keep track of what others do, such as tasks completed, time spent away from work station, hours worked, etc., so that I can prove that I'm working harder than they are.
		X			I don't think anyone should get something for nothing; I seldom do things for others unless I can get something later in return.
		X			I generally don't trust people I haven't worked with; I expect people to earn my trust.
	X				I go out of my way to do favors for my superiors so that I can cash in later on promotions and pay increases.
0	1	4	0	0	*Multiply the number of responses in each column by the score at the top of the column. Then record your score in the space provided in this row.*
TOTAL = 5					*Record your total score for this behavior here.*

Scoring the Frequency of Your Responsibility-Inhibiting Behaviors

VERBALLY ATTACKING					
0	**1**	**2**	**3**	**4**	**0 = Never 1 = Seldom 2 = Sometimes 3 = Often 4 = Always**
					If I really need to get someone's attention, I might speak with a harsh tone of voice and even shout.
					If I have to, I'll get into someone's personal space, stare, or put my finger in their chest to get my point across.
					When I think someone's ego is getting too big, I sometimes use sarcasm to bring them down a notch.
					In order to get someone to back down, if I have to, I will use personal insults.
					Multiply the number of responses in each column by the score at the top of the column. Then record your score in the space provided in this row.
TOTAL =					*Record your total score for this behavior here.*

KEEPING SCORE					
0	**1**	**2**	**3**	**4**	**0 = Never 1 = Seldom 2 = Sometimes 3 = Often 4 = Always**
					I mentally keep track of what others do, such as tasks completed, time spent away from work station, hours worked, etc., so that I can prove that I'm working harder than they are.
					I don't think anyone should get something for nothing; I seldom do things for others unless I can get something later in return.
					I generally don't trust people I haven't worked with; I expect people to earn my trust.
					I go out of my way to do favors for my superiors so that I can cash in later on promotions and pay increases.
					Multiply the number of responses in each column by the score at the top of the column. Then record your score in the space provided in this row.
TOTAL =					*Record your total score for this behavior here.*

					FINDING FAULT
0	**1**	**2**	**3**	**4**	**0 = Never 1 = Seldom 2 = Sometimes 3 = Often 4 = Always**
					I don't think mistakes should be overlooked; if someone makes a mistake, they need to be held accountable.
					I expect the people who work with me regularly to know what I expect; if they don't, I let them know it's their fault.
					Whenever I feel someone is unfairly criticizing me, I usually counterattack, placing the blame where it really belongs, on them.
					When problems arise, I consider it my responsibility to point out who is at fault.
					Multiply the number of responses in each column by the score at the top of the column. Then record your score in the space provided in this row.
TOTAL =					*Record your total score for these actions here.*

					NEEDING TO BE RIGHT
0	**1**	**2**	**3**	**4**	**0 = Never 1 = Seldom 2 = Sometimes 3 = Often 4 = Always**
					Because I know my job and do my homework, my ideas are well thought-out, so I do everything I can to convince others to agree that I'm right.
					When someone is trying to push an idea that's not as good as mine, I'll interrupt and explain why my idea is better.
					I hate to admit it when I'm wrong—which is seldom if ever; so if I think I might be wrong, I change the subject.
					I don't hesitate to use guilt, if necessary, to persuade others to do what needs to be done.
					Multiply the number of responses in each column by the score at the top of the column. Then record your score in the space provided in this row.
TOTAL =					*Record your total score for these actions here.*

					REFUSING TO FORGIVE
0	**1**	**2**	**3**	**4**	**0 = Never 1 = Seldom 2 = Sometimes** **3 = Often 4 = Always**
					Sometimes I'm so upset about what someone has done to me, I get angry with them about small things.
					When someone has disappointed me more than once, I will remind them of it—so that they won't do it again.
					I refuse to forgive people who are not sorry, have not apologized, or have not made up for the past.
					Some people simply don't deserve forgiveness; nothing they can say or do will change that.
					Multiply the number of responses in each column by the score at the top of the column. Then record your score in the space provided in this row.
TOTAL =					*Record your total score for these actions here.*

					BEING PASSIVE-AGGRESSIVE
0	**1**	**2**	**3**	**4**	**0 = Never 1 = Seldom 2 = Sometimes** **3 = Often 4 = Always**
					I may let others I don't agree with make a suggestion, but I usually find a way to prove it won't work.
					When others suggest a change or an idea I don't like I sometimes pretend I don't understand it; eventually they get frustrated and give up.
					I sometimes pretend to be helpless or inept, so that others will do the things I don't like to do.
					I sometimes give the impression that I'm willing to go along with an idea, but I usually can find a way to make sure the idea fails.
					Multiply the number of responses in each column by the score at the top of the column. Then record your score in the space provided in this row.
TOTAL =					*Record your total score for these actions here.*

					CREATING DIVERSIONS
O	**1**	**2**	**3**	**4**	**0 = Never 1 = Seldom 2 = Sometimes** **3 = Often 4 = Always**
					In order to avoid issues I don't want to talk about, I sometimes move the conversation to safer topics like sports, family or the weather.
					When the discussion gets too close to sensitive issues, I try to either divert the conversation to another topic or withdraw from the conversation altogether.
					If others directly ask what's bothering me, I defend myself by telling them they're getting too personal.
					I don't like to talk about what's bothering me; I prefer to talk about "other people's" concerns.
					Multiply the number of responses in each column by the score at the top of the column. Then record your score in the space provided in this row.
TOTAL =					*Record your total score for these actions here.*

					PLAYING THE VICTIM
O	**1**	**2**	**3**	**4**	**0 = Never 1 = Seldom 2 = Sometimes** **3 = Often 4 = Always**
					Rather than risk disapproval by saying something others might not like, I often choose to remain silent.
					Although I'm sensitive to criticism from others, I often will voluntarily take the blame when things go wrong.
					I don't want to be accused of having a big ego, so when others try to give me a compliment I tend to downplay my contribution.
					I'm not comfortable with expressing anger; when I'm feeling angry, I tend to become emotional and withdrawn.
					Multiply the number of responses in each column by the score at the top of the column. Then record your score in the space provided in this row.
TOTAL =					*Record your total score for these actions here.*

					AVOIDING
0	**1**	**2**	**3**	**4**	**0 = Never 1 = Seldom 2 = Sometimes 3 = Often 4 = Always**
					I don't like interpersonal conflict, so even if a work relationship is not working, I prefer not to talk about it.
					I think that failure is to be expected and even celebrated, as members experiment with improving the systems.
					My coworkers sometimes tell me I need to change, but I don't need to change, they do.
					I find that when a workplace relationship is not working, in most cases it's just not worth the effort to try to improve it.
					Multiply the number of responses in each column by the score at the top of the column. Then record your score in the space provided in this row.
TOTAL =					*Record your total score for these actions here.*

					GIVING UP
0	**1**	**2**	**3**	**4**	**0 = Never 1 = Seldom 2 = Sometimes 3 = Often 4 = Always**
					When my boss or a coworker is angry with me, anything I do will only make that person even angrier, so I do nothing.
					When certain individuals attack or abuse me I just wait for the attack to be over so that I can get away from them.
					I've given up on a mutually respectful relationship with certain individuals I work with, so now I just go through the motions with them.
					I find ways to avoid contact with coworkers who don't like me. I find it is better just not to talk with them.
					Multiply the number of responses in each column by the score at the top of the column. Then record your score in the space provided in this row.
TOTAL =					*Record your total score for these actions here.*

Plotting the Frequency of Your Responsibility-Inhibiting Behaviors

FREQUENCY OF BEHAVIOR	Plot your scores on the chart below, marking your scores with an X. Then, connect the Xs, creating a Behavior Frequency Trend Line									
VERY HIGH Frequency of Responsibility-Inhibiting Behavior	16									
	15									
	14									
	13									
HIGH Frequency of Responsibility-Inhibiting Behavior	12									
	11									
	10									
	9									
LOW Frequency of Responsibility-Inhibiting Behavior	8									
	7									
	6									
	5									
VERY LOW Frequency of Responsibility-Inhibiting Behavior	4									
	3									
	2									
	1									
	0									
Responsibility-Inhibiting Behavior	Verbally Attacking	Keeping Score	Finding Fault	Needing to be Right	Refusing to Forgive	Passive-Aggressive	Creating Diversion	Playing the Victim	Giving Up	Verbally Attacking

Reducing Responsibility-Inhibiting Behaviors

Review your responsibility-inhibiting behavior scores, and determine which behaviors you'd like to work on reducing. Identify the specific situations that have tended to trigger these behaviors, and then write down the specific steps you plan to take to reduce the frequency of these responsibility-inhibiting behaviors.

Steps I plan to take to reduce Bullying Behaviors:

(1) Verbally Attacking

(2) Keeping Score

(3) Finding Fault

(4) Needing to be Right

(5) Refusing to Forgive

Steps I plan to take to reduce Learned Helplessness Behaviors:

(1) Being Passive-Aggressive

(2) Creating Diversions

(3) Playing the Victim

(4) Avoiding

(5) Giving Up

Steps my colleagues and I can take to challenge the current social contract and create a healthier work environment:

Part II

TAKE RESPONSIBILITY
FOR ENCOURAGING *EMERGENT LEADERS*

Ricardo Semler, the self-described "maverick" and CEO of Semco uses an exercise in leadership workshops he regularly conducts. He invites a group of volunteers to the stage to act out a survivor simulation in which they have crashed an airplane in the Himalayas. He appoints one of them as captain and then asks them to work out over the next twenty minutes what to do next. Each time that he conducts this exercise, a leader (never the captain he's appointed) emerges who begins organizing the survivors into groups: "one assigned to looking for water, the other to fixing the radio or signaling passing airplanes, the third to tending the injured, and so on."

Semler describes what happens next. He interrupts the group and asks them to act out another scenario, and as he describes it, "this time an activist environmental group that had heard that a large chemical plant was going to dump toxic waste into the river that afternoon. Almost immediately, someone would take over as leader, and it was never the same person who had led the plane crash survivors. ... These exercises reinforced my belief that leadership indeed depends on the situation. As circumstances change, leadership must change. A certain set of skills, instincts, and personality traits may be perfect today, and become useless tomorrow."

Semler observes: "At some point in the process, self-management takes over. Self-interest and the survival instinct kick in. The group coheres as its components start to function according to their unique skills tempered by experience. From then on leadership, beyond acting as catalyst, directing traffic, and playing honest broker when conflicts arise, is superfluous. Moreover, in my view, obtrusive and intrusive leadership becomes counterproductive by interfering with the free interplay of individual talent and interest."[20]

These self-selecting leaders, leaders who have the courage to step forward with the "skills, instincts and personality traits" at precisely the right time are what I call *Emergent Leaders*. These Emergent Leaders need not be a person called a manager or supervisor. Emergent Leaders can be anyone who has the knowledge and skills to fill a need that an individual or a group lacks. In short, Emergent Leaders step forward to share their skills and experience whenever leadership is needed.

Emergent Leaders do five key things which enable them to take leadership at the appropriate time. They: (1) Coach, (2) Offer Counsel, (3) Connect People to Resources, (4) Encourage Stewardship, and (5) Help Others See the Big Picture.

Emergent Leaders *Coach*

In a Responsibility Culture, when a person needs to learn something new, to gather information, or develop expertise and master new skills and proficiencies, an Emergent Leader steps up to offer coaching.

Emergent Leaders *Offer Counsel*

Once people turn their attention toward solving job-related problems and making day-to-day workplace decisions, Emergent Leaders make themselves available to offer counsel so that people can find their own solutions to everyday issues and problems.

Emergent Leaders *Connect People to Resources*

Having learned how to make decisions and solve problems independently people in a Responsibility Culture begin to seek the resources they need to complete projects independently. Emergent Leaders connect their coworkers to the resources they need to meet these challenges.

Emergent Leaders *Encourage Stewardship*

Having mastered the art of securing resources, people are ready to assume ownership for their jobs and for the systems within which they work. Emergent Leaders encourage their coworkers to become stewards of the organization.

Emergent Leaders *Help Others See the Big Picture*

Every member of in a Responsibility Culture needs to understand how his or her job supports the larger purpose of the organization. To help make this important link, Emergent Leaders help their colleagues see the big picture by understanding how their individual and combined efforts contribute to the organization's success.

FOUR
EMERGENT LEADERS ARE COACHES

■ **IN THIS CHAPTER:**

Utilize the *More and Less Coaching Model*
Challenge Conventional Assumptions about Coaching
Apply the Emergent Leader Coaching Guidelines

In a world where the pace of change is accelerating, where new ideas, new products and new ways of doing things has become the norm, expanding one's knowledge and skills is essential. Books, articles, on-line resources, and classroom instruction are all effective avenues toward learning. In spite of these helpful sources, when you are on the job, there is no substitute for finding a good coach—someone who not only already possesses knowledge, skill and experience, but who is able to effectively transfer this information to others in a way that others can understand and act upon. To illustrate this, let me share another personal story.

Several years ago I was inspired to take up the game of golf. Although the pros I watched on TV could blast the ball 300 yards down the center of the fairway with relative ease, chip onto the green with deadly accuracy, and sink puts from several feet away, I found all of these seemingly simple skills incredibly difficult to master. I tried learning the game by subscribing to a popular golf magazine, hitting hundreds of balls at the practice range, and playing as often as I could on a little "executive" (par 3) course near my home. Still, after months of trying to learn on my own, not only was I not improving, my game was getting worse. As I now like to joke, I wanted to learn to play golf in the worst way, and by trying to teach myself I got my wish.

Finally I concluded that I needed some coaching, so I drove out to a nearby public course and signed up for some private lessons. To my dismay, I found that I had acquired a number of very bad swing habits which my golf instructor tried to help me discard and replace, with limited success. One day I was relating my golfing woes to a good friend—describing my

60

nasty slice off the tee, my tendency to badly hook my fairway shots, my wholly unreliable chipping, and, of course, the piéce de résistance: my habit of three-putting nearly every green. He suggested that I contact Ted, a golf coach who had helped him.

At my first lesson, Ted asked me to hit a few balls. After topping, chunking, slicing, and hooking a few shots, I expected him to tell me it was hopeless. Instead, over the next several weeks, Ted patiently helped me improve my golf swing. At each lesson, we focused on just one small adjustment that he wanted me to make, and over the course of the season, I was able to build a swing that significantly improved my golf scores. Ted isn't an effective coach because he is a fine golfer (which he is). He is effective because he possesses the coaching skills to transfer his knowledge of how to hit a golf ball to others. He often uses what we at *Responsibility Cultures* call: "The More and Less Coaching Model."

Utilize the *More and Less Coaching Model*

The More and Less Coaching Model is a process that begins by recognizing a teachable moment and continues until the person has mastered the new skill. Here's how a coaching session using the More and Less Coaching Model on the job might sound:

> "Mary, it looks to me like you're really struggling with operating that machine. I can sure understand how you feel, most people new to that machine have struggled with it the first time they've tried to use it. If I may coach you, I have some ideas that I think might help you out."
>
> "Well, Bob, I thought I was ready to handle this machine on my own after you and I worked together on it yesterday, but you're right, I'm having a tough time with it today. I'd sure appreciate your help."
>
> "I'd be glad to help, Mary. Let me offer a couple of tips based on what I've observed just in the last few minutes since I stopped by to see how you were doing.
>
> "First, I'd suggest that you be a little less concerned about the number of units you're producing right now while you're still learning how to operate the machine. It will take a while before you'll be producing the same number of units as the experienced operators.
>
> "Second, I suggest you spend a little more time making sure the new materials being added to the staging bin are lined up correctly. I think doing that

should stop the machine from jamming. Why don't you give it a try right now?"

With Bob's help, Mary clears the jam and places the materials in the staging bin. She restarts the machine and carefully monitors the machine's output. After a few minutes she adds material to the staging bin, and the machine jams again.

The *More and Less Coaching Model*

I. Recognize a teachable moment

II. Empathize with the learner

III. Make an offer to coach

IV. Coach: I suggest *more of …* / I suggest *less of …*

V. Check with the learner on the effectiveness of the coaching points

---

"Mary, the machine was humming along just fine. What do you think happened?"

"I think it had something to do with the material I added to the staging bin."

"Right you are! Now what do you think needs to change?"

"Oh, I remember now! When I add material to the staging bin I have to check that the leading edge of the material matches up perfectly with the material already in the bin, right?"

"Right again, Mary! Why don't you do that and let's see what happens."

Mary clears the jam, aligns the material in the staging bin and starts the machine again. Bob observes as Mary adds material to the staging bin three more times. She is careful to make sure that the leading edge of the new material matches up perfectly with the material already in the bin and no more jams occur.

"Looks like you've got it under control, Mary. I hope you found my coaching helpful. If you have any more trouble, call me on my cell, okay?"

"You've been a great help. I'll call if I get stuck again; and Bob, thanks!"

It's important to note that the coach should offer no more than one more and one less tip at a time (a little more of this and little less of that). Many coaching sessions are unsuccessful because the coach gives the person being coached too much information all at once. To teach a complex task, a good coach breaks the coaching down into a series of small steps, each of which can be understood and acted upon by the person being coached without confusion.

The More and Less Coaching Model allows the person being coached to process and practice each small step until he is successful. It also allows the coach to zero in on the specific areas where the person being coached needs the most practice. Of course, complex skills often require multiple coaching sessions, allowing the person being coached the time (often a day or more) to master the step he has learned before tackling the next step in the skill.

The true measure of a successful coaching session is a person who is able to understand and apply what he or she has learned, and to repeat the new skill successfully in the future independently.

Challenge Conventional Assumptions About Coaching

In conventional top-down work cultures, coaching is something quite different from my experience with my golf coach Ted, or Bob's coaching session with Mary. This is because in conventional cultures, coaches are operating under a different set of assumptions. Let's compare these assumptions.

Conventional Coaching Assumption: It's the boss's job to provide most of the coaching.

Emergent Leader's Coaching Assumption: It's everyone's job to offer coaching whenever they spot a person in a "teachable moment." It's also everyone's job to seek out coaching whenever they need help learning or mastering a new skill.

In conventional business cultures, as in sports, coaches are in is a position of power. Because most sports coaches are working with developing athletes who are young men and women striving to master their sport, coaches are authority figures. The coach plans and runs practices, choose who plays and who doesn't, and in many sports, provides instruction and direction during the course of competition itself. Coaches in conventional business cultures are also authority figures. They write the business plans, manage operations, choose which workers get the plumb assignments and which don't, and provide direction on a day-to-day or perhaps hour-to-hour basis. If there is coaching to be done, they do it.

In a Responsibility Culture, being a coach is not limited to persons in a position of authority. Instead, coaching can be offered by anyone with knowledge and skills that will benefit others who are in a "teachable moment." A teachable moment is that moment when you're ready to be receptive to coaching—ready to hear and act on the information and direction a coach can provide. The best way to alert a potential coach that you're at a teachable moment is to simply ask for coaching when you need it. To not ask for coaching when you really need it is a major violation in a Responsibility Culture.

Emergent Leaders learn to look for and respond to coworkers who indicate that they've reached a teachable moment. As illustrated in Ricardo Semler's story about his leadership workshops, Emergent Leaders tend to emerge in a group when it is struggling with a challenging new task. As frustration begins to become evident, or as the group appears to be struggling, an Emergent Leader often emerges to coach the group.

> *Conventional Coaching Assumption:* The boss's coaching is the most accurate and useful.

> *Emergent Leader's Coaching Assumption:* Accurate and useful coaching is available from virtually anyone.

In conventional organizations, one of the assumptions is that a boss has the most skill and knowledge of anyone in the work group; and therefore the boss's coaching is the most accurate and useful for people on the front lines. In fact, superior knowledge and skill are frequently the primary criteria for being promoted in a conventional top-down culture. This is not so in a Responsibility Culture where useful coaching is available from virtually anyone who possesses the knowledge you lack and the coaching skills to pass them along to you. While a leader in a Responsibility Culture may possess superior knowledge and job skills, it is much more important that he or she possess the leadership skills necessary to effectively coach. In fact, in a Responsibility Culture, one of the most highly valued leadership responsibilities that the organization looks for in aspiring leaders is exceptional coaching skills.

Conventional Coaching Assumption: It's the boss's job to improve individual performance during formal performance appraisals.

Emergent Leader's Coaching Assumption: Formal performance appraisals, because they happen infrequently, tend to have a negative impact on individual performance. In order for coaching to be effective, it must be provided immediately at a teachable moment.

In a culture where the belief is that one of a manager's or supervisor's main jobs is to assess and appraise the work output of subordinates, formal performance appraisals are considered a key tool. The focus is evaluating individual performance, as well as the performance of each business unit. In some organizations, someone other than a direct supervisor, like a coworker or internal customer, appraises performance. The purpose of a performance appraisal may be to decide on promotions or raises, to assist in career development, to set and measure goals, and to provide other kinds of performance feedback.

Unfortunately, there is significant evidence that performance appraisals do not work. As Tom Coens and Mary Jenkins, authors of *Abolishing Performance Appraisals* put it, "Due to its inherent design flaws, appraisals produce distorted and unreliable data about the contribution of employees. Consequently, the resulting documentation is not useful for staffing decisions and often does not hold up in court. Too often, appraisal destroys human spirit and, in the span of a 30-minute meeting, can transform a vibrant, highly committed employee into a demoralized, indifferent wallflower who reads the want ads on the weekend."[21]

This conclusion is based on more than fifty years of academic studies, industry surveys and professional articles.

However, feedback offered without judgment can be very useful, provided the person receiving the feedback initiates it and has complete control of the feedback received, and complete freedom to make use of the feedback in any way he or she chooses. In a Responsibility Culture, everyone is encouraged to take responsibility for getting feedback that will best serve their specific needs and situation.

Conventional Coaching Assumption: The boss's main purpose for coaching is to motivate people to improve.

Emergent Leader's Coaching Assumption: People must find their own motivation to improve; when people ask for coaching, they are already motivated and ready to learn and grow.

In conventional cultures, the assumption has been that it's the boss's job to motivate people to improve, as if people not in positions of leadership are somehow lacking a desire to improve. Once again, current research shows that the key to individual motivation lies not in "extrinsic" rewards like money and recognition. It lies in the "intrinsic" rewards like pride in a job well done and a sense that you're really making a difference.

In a Responsibility Culture, people decide for themselves when they're ready to learn and grow, and ready to ask for coaching. This form of self-management is a key component of intrinsic motivation. Part of being accountable is becoming very aware of one's need to learn, and to take the initiative to ask for coaching.

Conventional Coaching Assumption: The boss should offer coaching to help people address their weaknesses.

Emergent Leader's Coaching Assumption: Coaching people on how to address their weaknesses is not as effective as building on a person's strengths.

Emergent Leaders understand that helping people to improve on their weaknesses is a necessary element of coaching, but not as effective as building on a person's strengths. This is because in most cases these "weaknesses" stem from either a lack of natural aptitude, or a lack of interest in acquiring or improving a particular skill. If someone lacks the natural talent or aptitude for a skill, his or her efforts to improve will likely prove fruitless no matter how much effort is put forth. Likewise, coaching a person with low aptitude most often proves to be a waste of time and energy for the coach.

A lack of interest in learning or improving a skill can come from a number of sources. It's possible that the individual may be bored with the activity and thinks that improving his or her skills will do little to relieve the boredom. It's also possible that the individual recognizes his or her lack of aptitude for the skill, and therefore expects very little improvement from investing additional time and effort. A much better strategy is to build on a person's strengths, on their natural talents and interests. People are much more likely to invest great effort in activities that they believe will yield rewarding results.

Apply the Emergent Leader Coaching Guidelines

As I've already explained, Emergent Leaders look for a "teachable moment" before offering to coach. That's the moment when someone appears to be ready and receptive to coaching. Often this occurs after someone has struggled a bit with a new task or skill and either stalled or is beginning to show some level of frustration. While allowing someone to struggle a bit before offering coaching is generally a good idea, an Emergent Leader is sensitive enough to make the offer to coach before a coworker is ready to give up. Teachable moments are very individual; they are unique to each person. Some people are very open to coaching. Others may be overly dependent on their coach. And others may be very resistant to coaching, even when they are struggling. Asking permission with a question like, "May I offer some coaching?" shows respect for the person. Asking for permission before beginning to coach gives the person who appears to be at a teachable moment the element of control. This allows that person to choose whether or not they are ready or receptive to coaching. When offering to coach, Emergent Leaders do so as a friend and colleague, rather than as an authority figure (even if the coach is a person in authority.) The objective is to avoid any resistance to authority or resistance because of embarrassment or insecurity.

Emergent Leaders are willing to coach anyone who asks for help, regardless of rank or role. The focus is on providing coaching that will help the other person improve their skills and proficiencies. Emergent Leaders are also willing to ask for coaching whenever they need help. Every person in an organization, even the most experienced among us can learn from coworkers. Even when one's training and experience are high, sometimes the coaching of another Emergent Leader is helpful simply because their point of view differs from one's own. This is particularly true when it comes to how to best work with other teammates or customers with whom we may be having trouble relating. There simply is no one "best way" to deal with people; sometimes we benefit from being open to coaching from others on how to improve interpersonal exchanges. We need to be open to coaching from anyone who offers to help without becoming defensive. The key is to listen to and act on coaching tips with a willingness to learn.

THE EMERGENT LEADER COACHING GUIDELINES

Guidelines for Coaching

I. Look for a coachable moment before offering to coach.

II. Ask for permission before beginning to coach.

III. Offer coaching as a colleague, not as a superior.

IV. Be willing to coach anyone who asks for help.

Guidelines for Being Coached

I. Ask for coaching whenever you need help.

II. Be open to coaching from anyone who offers to help without becoming defensive.

III. Listen to and act on coaching tips with a willingness to learn.

IV. Give your coach feedback by asking clarifying questions.

Summary

Effective coaching begins by recognizing a teachable moment. Good coaches offer only one more tip and one less tip at a time so that the person can process the information and put it into practice independently. Emergent Leaders assume the following about coaching: (1) It is every person's job to offer coaching whenever they spot a person in a "teachable moment." It's also everyone's job to seek out coaching whenever they need help learning or mastering a new skill. (2) Accurate and useful coaching is available from virtually anyone. (3) Formal performance appraisals tend to have a negative impact on individual performance. In order for coaching to be effective, it must be provided without judgment at a teachable moment. (4) People must find their own motivation to improve; when people ask for coaching, they are already motivated and ready to learn and grow. (5) Coaching people on how to address their weaknesses does little to improve performance; building on a person's strengths is a much more effective coaching strategy.

FIVE
EMERGENT LEADERS OFFER COUNSEL

Offer Counsel Using the *Three-Stage Counseling Model*

Heather graduated from her college in Boston with a degree in management. Even before she graduated from college, she began testing her management skills for an exclusive downtown spa, an upscale florist, and a music software company. When she moved cross-country to San Francisco, she parlayed her experience into good-paying jobs eventually becoming the manager of a full-service spa which employs about thirty people.

Since beginning her management career, Heather has seldom hesitated to pick up the phone and call her mentor, Beth. Heather and Beth have been partners in problem solving by talking through Heather's issues together and discussing her alternatives, weighing the pros and cons of each option. Beth avoids giving Heather advice. Instead, she spends a good deal of time asking questions, listening, and reflecting what she hears. This allows Heather the freedom to choose her own solutions and to take responsibility for the outcome of her decisions.

When you have skills and knowledge that might benefit others, it's important to look for mentoring opportunities. Yet, because mentoring requires a long-term commitment, it is equally important to enter into mentoring relationships carefully, asking permission to mentor and offering to mentor as a partner, not as a person in authority. Likewise, when seeking a mentor, choose someone who shows a willingness to put your interests ahead of his or her own. Look for someone who has the time to mentor and is clear about what he or she has to contribute to the relationship and who will treat you as a peer.

Like Heather's mentor Beth, a good counselor employs a number of subtle skills including listening, asking questions, and providing feedback. The *Three-Stage Counseling Model* provides a good model for doing all three. Stage I is the Inquiry Stage, Stage II is the Counseling Stage, and Stage III is the Debriefing Stage.

THE THREE-STAGE COUNSELING MODEL

I. The Inquiry Stage
(a) Open-Ended Questions (b) Restating

II. The Counseling Stage
(a) Observations (b) Counseling

III. Debriefing Stage
(a) Next Steps (b) Counseling Feedback

I. The Inquiry Stage

(a) *Open-Ended Questions:* "What is the problem as you see it, Heather?"

Inquiry begins by asking open-ended questions, questions that can't be answered with a yes or a no. The precise wording of an open-ended question can vary considerably and need not be in the form of a question, as long as it gets Heather talking about her issue or problem. For example, Beth might say, "Tell me what happened." Beth might follow up with other open-ended questions like: "So, how do you think your coworker would describe this problem?" or "Is there another way to look at this problem?"

(b) *Restating:* "Heather, I hear you saying …"

Periodically restating accomplishes a number of purposes. First, restating reassures Heather that she is being heard, which encourages her to continue talking. Second, it gives Heather an opportunity to correct and clarify Beth's restatements. Third, restating, like looking into a mirror, helps Heather reflect on and clarify her thoughts and feelings. Fourth, restating is a wonderful tool for helping Heather when she may be rambling or caught up in emotions; it helps her to refocus and get back on track. Of course, if Beth over-uses restatement as a tool, she begins to sound like a parrot; or worse, gives Heather the impression that she is being ridiculed or belittled.

II. The Counseling Stage

(a) *Observations:* "Heather, here's my take on the problem you've described …"

During the counseling stage, Beth tries to make her observations as objective and non-judgmental as possible. Beth describes the problem as she sees it and gives an assessment of the magnitude and scope of each of the issues. Beth's observations might include how Heather might be contributing to the problem and other issues Heather might not have considered.

(b) *Offering Counsel:* "Heather, have you considered …?"

The goal of offering counsel is to help Heather find her own solution, not to offer a solution. It's not really important that the solution Heather chooses is, in Beth's opinion, a great solution or even a good solution. It's important that the solution might work. Once again, the key psychological element is—choice. Studies have shown that average solutions developed and implemented by the persons working to solve a problem outperform brilliant solutions developed by someone else.[22]

Part of human nature is that we take pride and ownership in our own creations and are far less invested in the creations of others. Put another way, when Heather chooses how to solve a problem, she'll find a way to make it work.

III. The Debriefing Stage

(a) *Next Steps:* "So, now that we've talked the problem over, and we've discussed possible solutions, Heather, what are your next steps?"

The idea, during the debriefing stage, is to help Heather arrive at a specific course of action. Beth continues to ask "next step" questions until both Beth and Heather are clear about what to do and confident that the solution has a chance to work. Talking through next steps gives Heather confidence to give the solution she's chosen a try. It may also be appropriate for Heather and Beth to agree on whether and how Heather might report back to Beth on the outcome of implementing her solution, so that together they can talk about lessons learned and/or possible additional next steps.

(b) *Counseling Feedback:* "Was my counsel helpful, Heather?"

Although the main focus of offering counsel is on helping Heather find a solution to her issue, it's also important that Beth elicit some feedback on whether or not the counseling session was helpful, and if not, why not. Every person who offers counsel has a favorite style, one that fits his or her personality and problem-solving process. Beth's style and process may not meet Heather's needs completely. Heather may be looking more for emotional support (without directly asking for it) rather than specific problem-solving ideas. Beth may be distracted by the issue itself or may not pick up on subtle, non-verbal cues given by Heather. It would be a good idea for Beth to ask something like, "Heather is there anything I could do differently that would be helpful the next time we talk about an issue?"

Use *Shared Values* as a Tool for Offering Counsel

Jill Wright and Sarah Fanning had been fuming at each other for more than a week. While they had been close friends and coworkers for more than seven years, they had recently stopped talking to each other.

It all started when a machine on the production line they jointly supervised had experienced a major breakdown. Production was stopped completely for more than six days while they waited for a part to be shipped from the supplier in Germany. Then it was another twenty hours before repairs could be completed.

Needless to say, management was not happy. The union contract required that the eighteen workers assigned to the line on both the day shift (Jill's crew) and swing shift (Sarah's crew) be temporarily "reassigned" to other production crews rather than be laid off. Since the workers weren't really needed elsewhere, it meant carrying significant payroll costs without much real return on investment. Worse, because the company was unable to deliver on time, their customer had cancelled the contract and moved their business to a competitor.

Senior management wanted to know why the breakdown had occurred—whether the machine had been improperly maintained, and/or whether the operators or shift supervisors had in any way been negligent.

Feeling the pressure to avoid blame, the finger pointing between Jill and Sarah began almost immediately and had degenerated quickly into a "war of silence" between the two.

Truth

Sharing the truth is not always easy. It is particularly difficult to share the truth when the truth is bad news or when there is genuine disagreement over what the truth really is. As human beings we share an intense need to preserve our own sense of righteousness when something has gone wrong. That is, we don't want to admit or believe that we might be a cause in a problem or issue, so we resort to slanting our version of the truth to make us look good or to make someone else look bad. Our identity is at stake, and we'll do almost anything to protect it. Is it any wonder, then, that when difficulty strikes we look for a scapegoat?

An Emergent Leader can be of great help in uncovering or sorting out "the truth" without resorting to scapegoating. As each player in the drama shares his version of the story, an Emergent Leader can help each person see that there may indeed be more than one valid version of "the truth." An Emergent Leader can also help the players explore and understand the feelings involved and to recognize that feeling are an important part of the truth.

> After waiting a few days for Jill and Sarah to work it out on their own, their boss, Carol Henley, called them into her office. Ms. Henley began the discussion by asking each of them, one at a time, to share their stories about what happened without comment or interruption from the other.
>
> As expected, both Jill and Sarah had very different stories to tell about what had happened, and each expressed hurt feelings toward the other. Now it was up to Carol to help Jill and Sarah to sort out what had happened and, more importantly, to find a way to fix the problem and move forward.

Trust

Building and sustaining trust requires effective two-way communication. We extend trust to our coworkers by allowing them to choose to take on responsibilities and to carry out agreements and promises. When trusting others, we need to be clear about our expectations and courageous enough to ask for help when we need it. Yet, people often lack the courage to trust without the help of an Emergent Leader. When communication breaks down, it often takes a third party, an Emergent Leader, to get communication flowing again and rebuild trust.

> As Carol expected, both Jill's and Sarah's initial versions of the story emphasized their own blamelessness in the situation and implied the other's culpability in the breakdown. Carol's patient prompting helped Jill and Sarah to begin to open up to each other. They saw that each of them had a share in the blame because they had each failed to communicate effectively regarding machine maintenance prior to the breakdown.
>
> Carol added that she felt she had a share of the responsibility for the breakdown. "My intention was to give you both space to manage your own crews by not hovering over you. I realize now that I had actually abandoned you both by failing to provide adequate support."
>
> As the discussion continued they discovered that there had been a breakdown in communication about expectations as to who was responsible for implementing the maintenance schedule.

Mentoring

Mentoring is a great way to share knowledge and experience. Fortunately it doesn't have to always be a one-way conversation; that is, mentoring flowing from a senior, more experienced person to a protégé. Mentoring is available to everyone at every level of experience—from colleagues more experienced than ourselves and from those who can offer us a fresh perspective, like new members of the organization and younger colleagues. Mentoring is not the exclusive role of supervisors, managers and senior workers. In fact, a manager or supervisor might put a mentor and protégé together when the two might not have otherwise found each other.

> Carol suggested that Jill and Sarah seek out the help of an experienced supervisor from another crew, Lori Brinkerhoff. Ms. Brinkerhoff had been instrumental in designing and implementing a continuous improvement system or her crew that had significantly reduced waste and improved quality output.
>
> Carol felt that Brinkerhoff's experience with examining workflow issues, and could help Jill's and Sarah's crews develop a workable maintenance schedule quickly, and as an added bonus, teach the basics of continuous process improvement.

Receptivity

Receptivity to new ideas is the key to improving workflow, to solving problems, and to meeting the unique needs of each customer. Emergent Leaders help coworkers to be receptive to new ideas by examining their preconceived ideas and prejudices and opening them up to exploring new ideas and finding new solutions to old problems.

When Ms. Brinkerhoff was brought in, she shared with Jill and Sarah the success her crew had experienced. Initially, Jill's and Sarah's crews were wary. They were concerned that "continuous process improvement" was simply a new way to point the finger of blame at them. Soon, with Lori's gentle coaxing, they began to examine their processes.

Gradually both Jill and Sarah's crews were able to see the wisdom of frontline production workers having the authority and responsibility for improving the system. With Lori's help, they began to test their ideas.

Taking Personal Risks

For an organization to remain vital and competitive in the marketplace, it needs people who have the courage to act on their beliefs and to step forward with new ideas, whether these ideas are popular or not. Emergent Leaders are instrumental in helping to create a risk-taking environment, helping to establish an environment where new ideas can be brought forward and examined without prejudice, an environment where it is safe to challenge the status quo without fear of reprisal.

> After Lori left, each of the crews began to experiment independently with improvements during their respective shifts. But without Lori's mentoring, workers began to slowly shift back into their old mode of thinking, afraid they would be blamed for their experiment's failures.
>
> With Carol's support and encouragement, Jill and Sarah gently confronted these old behaviors by making it clear that it was safe to experiment, and that it was even safe to fail! Gradually, with Carol's, Jill's and Sarah's support, workers gradually showed a greater willingness to step forward with their ideas and to experiment.

Giving Credit

All human beings have the need to be recognized and feel appreciated for what they contribute. Recognizing the contributions of coworkers provides a foundation of fairness in the organization that helps fuel the fire of personal motivation. It helps keep people enthusiastically engaged in their work and with each other. Emergent Leaders need not become cheerleaders in order to give credit where it is due; they can help this process by simply bringing individual and group contributions to light so that their efforts and results are acknowledged.

> Jill and Sarah were quick to recognize the contributions of individuals who had the courage to step forward with a new idea. They were especially careful to avoid blaming anyone when problems surfaced and they discouraged crew members from blaming each other for failures. Rather, Jill and Sarah regularly recognized people who volunteered ideas and found ways to improve the system. Jill and Sarah reminded their crews of what Deming had taught: that 95 percent of the problems they were experiencing were a result of the system, not people.

Honesty

For staff and customers, honesty and ethics in all matters provide a foundation of trust and confidence in an organization and in each other. Ethical behavior includes putting in an honest day's work and doing one's best toward creating the highest level of quality service and quality products. Emergent Leaders often play the role of the conscience of an organization, challenging groups and individuals to examine their behaviors and actions to be sure that they are consistent with their stated values; in other words, that there is integrity between words and actions.

> Despite the liberal recognition of individuals who showed courage, or perhaps because of it, some members of each crew became jealous. They sometimes acted out in inappropriate ways, becoming argumentative, passive-aggressive or verbally attacking their courageous teammates.
>
> Although in the past Jill and Sarah might have privately complained about these bullying and learned helplessness behaviors, they wouldn't have done anything about them. Now, because the social contract had changed, they felt obligated to confront individuals who were inhibiting responsibility-taking.

Over time, their crews picked up on Jill and Sarah's example and began to confront each other's toxic behavior honestly. Slowly, these behaviors diminished as workers held each other to a higher standard.

Selflessness

Selfless behavior may seem an unrealistic expectation in an organizational setting, particularly in conventional organizations where internal competition is common. The truth is that unless customers and colleagues feel that we are considering their needs and that we are putting their interests ahead of our own, they will cease to do business with us. Offering counsel is an act of selfless behavior. Rather than giving advice or offering a solution, Emergent Leaders subordinate their own selfish needs and desires to the needs of those with whom they work.

As Jill's and Sarah's crews became more willing to confront each other, an interesting thing occurred. They began to focus on finding ways to help each other improve the system. This behavior became the group norm—something that every crew member engaged in and expected of each other.

Summary

Offering counsel begins with listening. Two effective counseling models used are the *Three Step Counseling Model* and the *Eight Shared Values*. Using these tools, *Emergent Leaders* don't offer advice or solutions; they help their coworkers find their own solutions to their work-problems and issues.

SIX
EMERGENT LEADERS CONNECT PEOPLE TO RESOURCES

■ **IN THIS CHAPTER:**
Help People Find Information
Help People Find More Time
Helping People Find Money for Projects
Help People Find Added Manpower

Once individuals have learned how to solve problems independently they begin seeking the resources necessary to solve problems. Then an Emergent Leader's responsibility is to help those individuals connect to the resources they need. There are typically four types of resources needed: information, time, money, and manpower.

Help People Find Information

There's an old saying that "information is power." This is because in conventional top-down cultures, the usual beliefs are that information should be shared only on a "need-to-know" basis, and all information should be considered confidential unless otherwise indicated. Why is information treated as confidential? Because, by controlling the flow of information, those at the top feel they are better able to directly control both activity and results. By limiting access to information, control-oriented leaders become the sole conduit through which all information flows; information is shared downward only with their explicit approval. Since information is often used to assign blame and mete out punishment, sharing the truth becomes dangerous. As a result, people up and down the chain of command often will tell their bosses what they want to hear. They'll manipulate the numbers in reports in order to avoid being blamed for bad news.

By contrast, in Cultures of Responsibility information is available to anyone who needs it. The rule of thumb is "no secrets," unless the information, for reasons of safety, security, legality, or fiduciary responsibility, needs to be confidential. By allowing information to flow freely, workers are able to solve problems, improve workflow, remove roadblocks, and respond to variations in customer demand quickly and efficiently without having to wait for approval. People in Cultures of Responsibility have access to two broad categories of information: *tactical information* needed for day-to-day tasks, and *strategic information* that provides the context for longer-term decision-making and problem solving. Strategic information allows people to "see the big picture" so that they understand how the work they are doing contributes to the organization's broader purpose.

In the mortgage industry, despite, or perhaps because of the recent issues in the credit market, there are a number of lenders who have made it possible for loan officers to make a decision on whether or not to make a loan without needing to submit the loan to a loan committee for approval. This is made possible in two ways. First, these organizations reach agreement on their loan approval criteria: the loan officers know precisely what kind of borrowers fit their lending risk profile and which borrowers are not qualified. Second, through the use of high-speed internet and intranet connections, the loan officers have access to credit history and other important data almost instantly. In the past, loan decisions were nearly always made by the loan committee, often composed of the senior executives. Now, because the criteria is made clear and financial information on individual borrowers is so freely available, the decision as to whether to make the loan can be made by individual loan officers.

Just making information available is not enough. Information must flow freely. To illustrate, a study conducted by GM in the 1990s provides us with insights into how differently GM and Toyota viewed the role of team leaders and how that impacts the flow of information:

> ■ Team Leaders at GM reported they spent only 52% of their time doing work on the shop floor, while team leaders at one of the Toyota plants spend 90% of their time directly involved with work on the shop floor. (Impact: Communicating what is going on is difficult if your team leader is gone half the time.)
>
> ■ 21% of the team leader's time at Toyota was spent filling in for workers who were absent or on vacation; GM leaders did this 1.5% of the time. (Impact: By filling in for front-line workers more often, team

leaders pick up a lot more information about how well the system is working more because they are observing the work first-hand.)

■ 10% of Toyota's team leader's time was spent ensuring a smooth flow of parts to the line. GM team leaders were at 3%. (Impact: Team leaders at Toyota are much more aware of inaccuracies of information that might affect the getting the right parts to the line and on time.)

■ 7% of the Toyota team leader's time was spent actively communicating job-related information. This was virtually absent at GM. (Impact: Front-line workers are much more aware of what's going on throughout the plant and with changes in customer demand.)

■ 5% of the Toyota team leader's time was spent observing the team working, in order to anticipate problems. This did not happen at all at GM.[23] (Impact: By directly observing the team working, supervisors at Toyota have unfiltered information about workflow, and as a result are able to make adjustments before problems occur.)

Even though GM was trying to implement Toyota management concepts, they clearly had failed to understand the team leader's role in enhancing the flow of information. Whereas Toyota has made their team leaders partners with workers on the floor, sharing in the work, helping the workers anticipate problems and improve workflow, and otherwise communicating job-related information.

Unfortunately, it appears that Toyota has regressed in this regard. The February 2010 Congressional hearing revealed that, perhaps in response to their rapid growth, Toyota has reverted to the same "command-and-control" model that has thwarted quality at GM and other American auto manufacturers. Under intense questioning, Toyota executives conceded that virtually all key decisions regarding manufacturing and safety are made in Japan. In direct opposition to the principles laid down by Taiichi Ohno when he established the *Toyota Production System (TPS)* in the 1930s, Toyota's current leadership has made the flow of information one-way. This migration toward a top-down management philosophy may be exactly the opportunity Toyota's competitors have been waiting for. According to the most recent J.D. Powers ratings of overall quality for GM is roughly equivalent to Toyota. Toyota has pledged to return to "regional information collection." Time will tell whether Toyota can successfully return to an effective two-way communication system and whether GM can integrate free flowing information systems that allow them to effectively compete and survive.

Help People Find More Time

In a fast-paced world where the pressure to perform accelerates daily, workers at every level of an organization feel the pressure to meet deadlines, complete projects, fulfill production quotas, and improve the systems. Yet, according to a survey published on HSalary.com, "the average worker admits to frittering away 2.09 hours per 8-hour workday, not including lunch and scheduled break-time."[24] If it's true that the average worker wastes more than a quarter of his time each day, what are they really saying when they ask for more time? In many cases, they're really asking to be relieved of tasks for which they see little or no value. Ask workers in a conventional top-down culture whether much of what they do is a waste of time—as dictated by their job descriptions or the systems within which they work—and they'll tell you, "Absolutely, ... but that's management's fault!"

However, when placed in a Responsibility Culture, these same workers are able to find the time they need by removing roadblocks and improving workflow; in short, they eliminate time-wasting tasks. In many cases, finding the time needed to solve a problem or complete a project is simply a matter of reordering priorities and putting less important tasks aside. An Emergent Leader may help coworkers find more time by filling in for them while he or she continues working on an important project that takes them away from their normal job duties.

At times, however, finding more time may require a temporary change in workers' job responsibilities. In this case, workers may need to negotiate with their colleagues. That is, workers may need to convince their coworkers who may not be as busy to take on some of their current job duties until they're able to complete the project or solve the problem. In a Responsibility Culture, this kind of give-and-take of job responsibilities happens all the time. This strategy tends to eliminate workers frittering away time by encouraging them to help out coworkers who are overloaded, knowing that they can expect the same help when they become busy.

Help People Find Money for Projects

In a Responsibility Culture, discussions about allocating more money for solving problems are not about offering an incentive, a pay increase, or a bonus. Money discussions are more likely to be about additional funds for operating or capital budgets. While the old saying "You can't solve a problem by simply throwing money at it" is true, of course, it could be that adding money to the budget may be justified—provided a business case for the request can be made for the additional funds.

Of course, no organization has unlimited funds and every organization is concerned about the wise allocation of financial resources. In a Responsibility Culture, Emergent Leaders step forward to help coworkers seeking resources to develop and present a business case explaining how the added expenditure will benefit customers and the organization. A business case may or may not be a formal written proposal. Regardless of the form of the proposal, a request for additional funds is submitted to the appropriate forum within the organization for approval. This might be to the leadership group within the team, or for larger expenditure, to the organization's Senior Executive Team.

Tom Peters, the well known author and management consultant, tells the story of a worker on the frontline at Harley-Davidson making a proposal to purchase a major piece of equipment for the shop floor. Being accustomed to seeing top-down environments where ideas come exclusively from the top, Peters is astonished to overhear the staff member telling a coworker that he's sweating over a proposal. Here is a staff member who has talked to vendors, run the numbers, and put together a business case for making a capital expenditure. Unlike conventional cultures where workers are told by management, "You don't get paid to think; now get back to work!" workers at Harley-Davidson routinely develop business cases for making changes they'd like to implement.[25]

Anticipating the occasional need for additional operating funds, some organizations pre-authorize a set amount of money that can be spent without prior approval. In some retail establishments, employees may be provided with a small budget of $500-$2,000 annually to appease unhappy customers. In this situation, the business case for the expenditure is made after-the-fact.

The main point regarding money as a resource is that everyone in a Responsibility Culture learns how to make a business case for additional funds or to simply use good judgment when additional spending is needed. Most times this can easily be handled by an individual or a small group of workers; at other times, developing a business case often requires the help of an Emergent Leader with financial skills and experience.

Help People Find Added Manpower

"I need some help!" How often have we heard these words from a coworker? Unfortunately, managers in conventional top-down cultures answer this cry for help by asking people to simply work harder. They try to improve productivity through short-term solutions such as demanding that people work longer hours and suspending vacation time. In the end these productivity-boosting strategies, while perhaps achieving short-term cost savings, do not and cannot result in sustainable gains in productivity. Experience has shown that people, when asked to work harder, may be able to increase their productivity for short periods of time. However, workers cannot sustain increased levels of productivity for an extended period without working smarter, improving processes and systems, or finding ways to eliminate waste.

Sometimes the volume of work simply exceeds the capacity of the people available for the tasks. At these times, shifting job responsibilities among the existing work force or asking team leaders to fill is inadequate; more workers are required. In this case the question is: Who do we let in? Where do we find the right people who are skilled, self-motivated and trustworthy enough to get the job done?

If you ask managers in conventional top-down cultures, they would tell you that good people are rare, that most people are average at best, or are more likely to be poor performers. Their experience tells them they're right, because most managers in these cultures find that ninety percent of their people significantly under-perform compared to their "A players." That's the reason the *Topgrading*[26] system seems justified. The point of "Topgrading" (also called "Forced Ranking") is to reward the top highly-productive ten percent for exemplary work, to encourage the middle moderately-productive eighty percent to improve their performance, and to eliminate (fire) the bottom poorly-productive ten percent. The problem with this kind of thinking is that it blames poor productivity on people, not on the system. (Remember, Deming proved that 95% of organizational problems are the result of the design of the systems.)

Topgrading fails to take into account the negative impact of such a competitive system on the majority of the workforce, particularly the middle eighty percent who are not being "rewarded." Of course, there are always a few who seem to thrive because of, or in spite of, an internally competitive environment; but most workers in highly competitive cultures wither under the constant pressure to improve. These organizations have a difficult time finding competent replacement workers for the bottom ten percent who are fired annually. Interestingly, organizations that have established a Responsibility Culture seem to have no difficulty finding good people who are thrive in a highly collaborative work environment.

Organizations that have successfully created a Responsibility Culture are able to, as Nordstrom management puts it, "achieve extraordinary results with ordinary people."[27] This is because the work environment is so radically different from conventional cultures. Organizations that believe in people taking responsibility screen for character first, skill and experience second. They look for and hire people who are values-driven, self-motivated, and are willing to take responsibility.

Summary

Emergent Leaders connect people to the resources of time, money, manpower, and information they seek. Finding the resources necessary to solve problems, remove roadblocks, improve workflow, and respond to variations in customer demand is the goal of connecting people to resources.

SEVEN
EMERGENT LEADERS ENCOURAGE STEWARDSHIP

■ **IN THIS CHAPTER:**

Encourage Job Ownership

Encourage Continuous Job Exploration

Encourage Shared Stewardship of the Systems

Peter Block, the highly respected author and consultant, describes stewardship as "the willingness to be accountable for the well-being of the larger organization."[28] In a Responsibility Culture, front-line workers are responsible for delivering customer value by both owning their jobs and owning the systems within which they work. Emergent Leaders partner with coworkers as stewards of the systems. Although stewards are most often not literally owners of the business, they think and act like owners.

Encourage Job Ownership

Perhaps the best example I've run across of a CEO who has completely turned over ownership of individual jobs to employees is Ricardo Semler of Brazil-based *Semco*. Semler gives people the freedom to choose what they'd like to do, the right to decide on their personal working hours, and even the authority to set their own salaries. Hard to believe? In doing business this way, Semco grew from $35 million in annual revenue, to $212 million in just six years. With more than 3000 employees they have virtually no turnover. Semler's philosophy of putting employee freedom and job satisfaction ahead of corporate goals has proven that it is possible to achieve incredible growth and profit that far exceed that of their competitors.

Consider the story of Auro Alves as told by Semler himself. "Auro Alves is a sales and technical-assistance manager at Semco. He began his career with us as a truck driver. He'd driven a bus in Sao Paulo before joining

Semco and expected that he'd spend his life as a heavy-duty commercial driver. Less than five months after coming to Semco, he moved into product acquisition, and eight months after that, took a job as a junior buyer. He got involved in union activities, (that's right, Semco is a *union* organization) discovered that he liked being a leader, and that other workers were comfortable with his management style, too. He had a knack for coming up with new ways of doing old tasks at Semco in order to involve more people.

"While at Semco, Auro has taken dozens of elective courses, including English, Spanish, computers, negotiation technique, sales methods, and customer care. He's had offers to work elsewhere, but turned them down because Semco allows him to grow. Auro isn't finished exploiting his own 'reservoir of talent.' He has a five-year plan of his own, even if the company frowns on them for itself. He owns a beach house in Peruibe and spends part of his seven-day weekend there fishing and getting to know the local people. (*Seven-Day Weekend* is the title of one of Semler's book.) He plans to move there one day and run his own 'virtual business' as a supplier or consultant to Semco."

At Semco, people like Auro are not only encouraged to develop their own job skills and to explore different job opportunities within the organization; they even determine their own salaries. There are no set salary systems within the company. Rather, each self-managed group decides what makes the most sense for them. This might include "fixed salaries, bonuses, profit sharing, commissions, royalties on sales, royalties on profits, commissions on gross margin, stock or stock options, IPO or sale." They allow groups to set their own salaries based on five factors: (1) external wage comparison survey data, (2) internal wage comparison data, (3) the market conditions that determine whether they can pay above or below the market, (4) what each individual would like to be making, and (5) what their spouses, neighbors and friends are making.

Of course, the last two factors are known only to each individual. The others are made known to the company employees. By making the first three factors known to employees, Cultures of Responsibility make each individual responsible for justifying his or her salary to coworkers. "Anyone who requests too large a salary or too big a raise runs the risk of being rejected by their fellow stewards—their colleagues. So, not too many people ask for excessive paychecks." Semler concludes his argument for allowing people to set their own salaries this way, "If workers understand the big picture, they'll know how their salaries fit into it." [29]

CEOs like Ricardo Semler and other organizations that have created a Responsibility Culture support job ownership because they understand how much taking this approach benefits both customers and the organization. Customers are happier because they are interacting with employees who, because they own their jobs, are willing and able to do what it takes to meet their unique needs. The executives of the company are happier because the company operates with far less waste and much better profitability.

Encourage Continuous Job Exploration

In order to successfully link responsibility with accountability, it's important that people have the freedom to explore, that is, to choose the tasks they're willing and able to take on. It's the element of choice that allows them to take on more responsibility. In a Responsibility Culture, people are given the freedom to negotiate with their coworkers to exchange or share job responsibilities. As the word implies, negotiating requires some give and take among the participants. This means that no one in the group is given the right to cherry-pick the best tasks leaving the worst chores to others. It also means that someone called a "boss" no longer assigns or delegates job tasks either. Instead, members in a Responsibility Culture decide together who will be responsible for each task.

The process works something like this: First the team reaches agreement on their reason for existence (purpose,) who their customers are, and what their customers need and want. Next, they list all of the important tasks for which the team is responsible and accountable. Then, they begin negotiating who in the group is willing and able to take on each task, including those responsibilities that might traditionally have been given to a supervisor (things like: planning, setting priorities and policies, and deciding who will do what each day.)

Negotiating job tasks is a dynamic process. Who does each job task changes over time as people gain the experience and knowledge they need to take on greater levels of responsibility and accountability. Other important negotiating issues include deciding how removing roadblocks and improving workflow will be done; how progress will be reported, to whom and how frequently; and how to keep the focus on delivering what customers value.

The goals of the job negotiation process are to (1) allow people to choose job responsibilities that are personally motivating, (2) allow every person to become self-managing, and (3) make sure that every member of the team understands exactly what he or she has agreed to be responsible for, and to whom they're accountable.

Here's Semco's approach to negotiating job responsibilities: "At Semco we don't dictate to people what their responsibilities are; we assume that as adults they can figure out for themselves what it takes to do their job and that without guidelines to adhere to, they're more likely to test the boundaries of what they do. … Without a formal job description, people can wander into neighboring work activities without being chased away for trespassing. … [Workers] have the freedom to decide for themselves what their job entails. They self-manage. They also control where they work, when they work and how much they are paid for their work."[30]

Semco's approach may seem too haphazard, but it's really not. It works really well because it taps into the intrinsic motivations of each person. As Semler correctly observes, "A great deal of employee satisfaction occurs when individuals have some leverage over the logistics of their jobs. … People don't come to work to produce an inferior product, to come late and leave early, to be bored and insubordinate. They work for a reason, for at least some kernel of interest that attracted them to their particular field or profession as a means of earning a paycheck."[31]

One of the goals of creating a Responsibility Culture is to give people the opportunity to rediscover a level of job satisfaction that they may have lost in a more conventional "managed" work environment. Giving people a high degree of control over their work lives is enormously important in reigniting full engagement in the jobs they've chosen. Although it may seem contradictory, in order for people to perform well in meeting the needs of customers, they need to be able to pursue their own self-interest. In other words, they need to be allowed to do work that they find personally motivating and satisfying. Put simply, people who feel trusted to pursue their own dreams put their hearts and souls into their work.

Encourage Shared Stewardship of the Systems

In conventional cultures, managers and supervisors are in charge of measuring their work group's results and the individual contributions of each member of the group (through annual performance reviews.) In a Responsibility Culture, however, people on the front-lines do most of the measuring using the Systems Thinking Measurement Criteria: (1) Measure only those things that relate to what customers values, (2) Measure only those things that help the team understand the systems and improve your ability to deliver customer value, and (3) Make the people responsible for doing the work responsible for doing the measuring.

(1) Measure only things that relate to what customers value.

Workers measure only those things that relate to what their customers value. For example, at a fast food restaurant, customers value speed and low cost the most; presentation and quality are secondary. In fast food restaurants that have established a Responsibility Culture, they create a system that will deliver what customers want from fast food restaurants: inexpensive food delivered quickly. They realize, of course, that in addition to speed and low cost, their customers also value presentation and quality, so they add playgrounds for the kids, comfortable, well-lighted dining areas, and clean restrooms.

In upscale restaurants, however, presentation and quality are what customers value most. So, in upscale restaurants that have established a Responsibility Culture, they create a system that shouts high quality from the moment their guests drive up. This might include valet parking; and a maitre d' dressed formally and addressing patrons as "sir" and "madam." The waiters probably wear black slacks or skirts, crisply starched white shirts, pressed aprons, and hair that is neatly groomed. Tables are most likely set with linen cloths, crystal-clear water goblets and wine glasses, and gleaming flatware. The entire dining experience is designed to appeal to the senses.

(2) Measure only those things that help the team understand the systems and improve your ability to deliver customer value.

Workers design measures that help them understand and improve the system's ability to deliver customer value. Would fast food and gourmet restaurants measure the same things? Yes and no. Because they're both in the restaurant business, there would be some things they both would measure, such as the amount spent per ticket and which items on the menu sell more. The difference is that the fast food restaurant would be very interested in measuring how long it takes to complete an order—with the goal of reducing the time customers have to wait. After all, customers choose fast-food restaurants because they want their food fast. On the other hand, the gourmet restaurant might be more interested in carefully monitoring every aspect of presentation: the ambiance of the dining room, the precise manners of the waiter, wine steward, server and table-busser, and how the food looks on the plate. To reiterate, each type of restaurant designs their food delivery system to provide more of what their customers' value, and the members of each self-managing team closely monitor how well their system delivers those things.

(3) Make the people responsible for doing the work responsible for doing the measuring.

The people who are doing the work do the measuring. In conventional cultures, the measuring is done either by a supervisor and/or an auditor. As I've explained earlier, this is based on the assumption that people's behavior and activity are the main issue, not the system design or the measurements themselves. People in a Responsibility Culture make a different assumption: problems are usually the result of the design of the system, not the people working within the system. This creates a level of accountability on the frontlines that is not possible in an authoritarian culture. Put simply, when people become stewards of the measurement systems, they are eager to step up and become stewards of the systems by continuously making sure that the systems are designed to respond to what customers want.

Summary

Emergent Leaders encourage stewardship by encouraging job ownership, encouraging job negotiations, and encouraging shared stewardship of the systems. People in a Responsibility Culture take ownership of the measurement systems measuring only what customers value, designing measures that will help them understand how to continuously improve the system, and doing the measuring themselves.

EIGHT
EMERGENT LEADERS HELP OTHERS SEE THE BIG PICTURE

■ **IN THIS CHAPTER:**

Create a Compelling Case for Change
Communicate the Responsibility-Taking Message
Overcome Complacency
Create a Real Sense of Progress toward Responsibility
Make a Responsibility Culture Stick

In his book, *Let My People Go Surfing,* Yvon Chouinard, founder and owner of Patagonia Inc., describes how he made the transition from a lone entrepreneur tinkering in his workshop with rock-climbing equipment to becoming the leader of an international manufacturer of environmentally friendly outdoor gear. Chouinard characterizes his story as "the education of a reluctant businessman." In the introduction of his book he describes the philosophy that has shaped his vision. Having grown up in the sixties, he had come to disdain big corporations and their "lackey governments," [i.e., conventional systems and structures.] "My values are a result of living a life close to nature." Chouinard sees himself as a "contrarian," taking the lessons learned from living an "alternative lifestyle" and applying them to running a business.

"My company, Patagonia, Inc., is an experiment. ...We believe the accepted model of capitalism that necessitates endless growth and deserves the blame for the destruction of nature must be displaced. Patagonia and its thousand employees have the means and the will to prove to the rest of the business world that doing the right thing makes for good and profitable business." Chouinard's vision is that of a company that "can break the rules of traditional business and make it not just work but work even better ..."[32]

Create a Compelling Case for Change

For Yvon Chouinard, change was called for when he realized one day that he wasn't merely an avid outdoorsman making equipment that others wanted to use. "I had always avoided thinking of myself as a businessman. I was a climber, a surfer, a kayaker, a skier, and a blacksmith." He continued the conversation to say that "One day it dawned on me that I *was* a businessman … It was also clear that in order to survive at this game, we had to get serious." After experiencing tremendous expansion for several years Patagonia was experiencing growing pains. "Looking back now, I see that we made all the classic mistakes of a growing company. We failed to provide the proper training for the new company leaders, and the strain of managing a company with eight autonomous product divisions and three channels of distribution exceeded management's skill. We never developed the mechanisms to encourage them to work together in ways that kept the over-all business objectives in sight." So Patagonia's Leadership Coalition began making the changes, and to communicate those changes to the whole organization.

One of the most important new trends in the twenty-first century is that the most successful organizations in the world are moving away from conventional management thinking toward a Responsibility Culture. CEOs are becoming keenly aware that the biggest threat to their organization is failing to make the change to a Responsibility Culture fast enough. Therefore, they spend a good deal of energy creating a sense of urgency in an effort to shake people out of their complacency. Leaders throughout these organizations challenge the status quo by articulating a compelling case for change, identifying the problems associated with continuing on the organization's present path and spelling out the advantages of establishing a Responsibility Culture.

It turns out that the leaders of organizations that have adopted a Responsibility Culture as an operation principle are not supermen or superwomen who do it all themselves. Rather, they enlist the support of a *Leadership Coalition* within the organization. Without the visible support of this Leadership Coalition, which includes senior leaders, middle leaders and front-line leaders who have become Emergent Leaders, the change to a Responsibility Culture is likely to fail. The Leadership Coalition helps to make the case for change in a number of ways: they model non-authoritarian leadership; they encourage people to experiment; they make sure people are able to get the training they need; and they encourage greater and greater levels of ownership. In short, this Leadership Coalition makes the case for moving to a Responsibility Culture by "walking the talk."

Communicate the Responsibility-Taking Message

Patagonia has moved aggressively to create a Responsibility Culture. Entrepreneurs within the company create products that solve the unique problems of outdoor enthusiasts like staying dry. "At a time when the entire mountaineering community relied on the traditional, moisture-absorbing layers of cotton, wool, and down, we looked elsewhere for inspiration—and protection." Creative thinkers at Patagonia developed the first polyester climbing sweater, and later designed climber's polypropylene underwear, which kept the climber both drier and warmer with fewer layers of clothing. With tough competitors who copied their designs, Patagonia has been able to maintain their competitive edge by getting Emergent Leaders to take responsibility for continuously improving their products, always looking for ways to deliver more of what their customers want.

Making the change to a Responsibility Culture requires effective communication. In order to win hearts and minds, people in the organization need to be introduced to the idea of taking responsibility and understand the path to get there. Sending a memo, giving a speech or publishing an article in the company newsletter is insufficient. People need time to interact and discuss this new way of doing things in both formal and informal meetings. Although meetings may be time consuming, costly and logistically difficult, bringing people together to process and discuss the new philosophy is very important. Time away from their regular jobs allows people on the front lines time to understand and accept the idea of owning their jobs so they can successfully take ownership for their jobs and for becoming Emergent Leaders.

Repetition of the message is important. Advertising firms understand this very well. They never place a single ad, they develop an ad campaign that targets an audience and repeats the message often and in many different media. Leaders understand as well that effective communication follows the old adage, "When you think they've got it, tell them again." They know that the new philosophy needs to be heard many times before it sinks in; and people need to hear from all members of the Leadership Coalition, not just the senior executives. Keeping in mind that actions speak louder than words, the behavior and actions of the entire Leadership Coalition must be consistent with the new responsibility-taking philosophy. When inconsistencies surface, and they will, they need to be addressed. It takes time for the organization's systems and structures to change. It becomes evident very quickly that conventional top-down operating systems are not designed to support a Responsibility Culture. The Leadership Coalition needs to acknowledge these inconsistencies and encourage the members to challenge them.

Overcome Complacency

Overcoming complacency is one the biggest obstacles to this change. There are many reasons for complacency. One reason is that people have seen change initiatives come and go, and most have failed to deliver results as promised. People have a good reason to be skeptical. Most change initiatives don't work, not because the ideas are necessarily invalid or poorly conceived, but because they get the change process backwards. They begin by trying to change the behavior of people rather than changing the system itself. It turns out that Deming was right, 95% of problems are caused by the system, not by people. So, establishing a Responsibility Culture focuses on changing the systems and structures rather than on changing people.

Chouinard understands the dangers of complacency very well. "After all those years of 30 percent to 50 percent compound annual growth and trying to have it all, Patagonia hit the wall." With the country in recession in 1991, dealers were cancelling orders, inventory grew, their credit line was significantly reduced, and Patagonia was forced for the first time in their history to lay people off, which they were loath to do. "We had never laid people off simply to reduce overhead. In fact, we had never laid anyone off for any reason. Not only was the company like an extended family, for many it was a family, because we had always hired friends, friends of friends, and their relatives." Finally they had to let 120 people go, which was 20 percent of the workforce. Like so many organizations before them, "We were forced to rethink our priorities and institute new practices." In short, they were shaken out of complacency and began to make real progress toward taking responsibility.

The Leadership Coalition needs to be prepared to break through significant obstacles and roadblocks to a Responsibility Culture. Not the least of these obstacles is the existing organizational structure. A conventional top-down organizational structure delegates responsibility downward and ensures accountability through a system of direct supervision, performance reports and periodic audits. The difference in a Responsibility Culture, is that everyone is expected to be both responsible and accountable to each other, to the organization, and most all to their customers. Breaking out of command-and-control thinking and the requisite need for layers of supervision and serial audits is a tremendous leap for leaders and workers who have lived in this kind of environment for most of their adult lives.

Create a Real Sense of Progress Toward Responsibility

Chouinard understands the importance of a sense of progress very well. As the company recovered from their brief business slow down, he decided to teach his employees part of what he had learned as a student of Zen philosophy. "In Zen archery, for example, you forget about the goal—hitting the bull's—eye and instead focus on all the individual movements involved in shooting an arrow. You practice your stance, reaching back and smoothly pulling an arrow out of the quiver, notching it on the string, controlling your breathing, and letting the arrow release itself. If you've perfected all the elements, you can't help hitting the center of the target. The same philosophy is true for climbing mountains. If you focus on the process of climbing, you'll end up on the summit. As it turns out, the perfect place I've found to apply this Zen philosophy is the business world."

In order to establish and keep up momentum and enthusiasm for the move toward a Responsibility Culture, people need to feel a sense of real progress and success. A good way to create a sense of real progress is to institutionalize the sharing of good news stories and discussions of lessons learned from failures through regularly scheduled *Application Meetings*. Application Meetings are an opportunity for all members of the organization to gather together in small groups to talk about how the organization is progressing toward a Responsibility Culture. During the initial stages of the change, these Application Meetings should be held monthly, so everyone in the organization has a chance to hear about what's happening in other parts of the organization.

Application Meetings should not be off the cuff or ad hoc. They need to be carefully planned in advance and presented by members of the Leadership Coalition. During each monthly meeting, a senior leader gives a brief view from the top. Then a mid-level leader teaches something that everyone in the organization needs to learn. Finally, a frontline Emergent Leader shares an *application issue* (a good news story or a failed experiment) and facilitates a discussion about lessons learned. In just ninety minutes, everyone in the organization hears what's going on from the senior leadership's perspective, learns something new, and has an opportunity to discuss how well the organization is applying the essential elements of a Responsibility Culture.

Make a Responsibility Culture Stick

Patagonia has always understood the importance of finding ways to make the Responsibility Culture stick. In 1991 the days of uncontrolled growth for Patagonia were over. They found they needed a new "models of stewardship and sustainability" against which to gauge their future progress. So they eliminated several layers of management and streamlined their systems. They adopted a controlled growth rate of about five percent a year and got serious about choosing raw materials for their clothing line that had the least damaging environmental impact. They were recognized for their turnaround, listed in *Working Mother* magazine as one of the "100 Best Companies to Work For," and in 2004 were ranked 14 in the "Top 25 Medium Sized Businesses" by the Great Place to Work® Institute and the Society for Human Resource Management.

Making a new Responsibility Culture stick requires making real changes from a culture of autocracy and bureaucracy to a culture of mutual trust and accountability. This requires time and persistence. People need time to internalize a Responsibility Culture, both in terms of the leadership model and organizational structure. Making this transition often requires *years*, not weeks or months. Even when people understand and accept the new concepts, changing the basis of relationships is a slow and sometimes painful process. Changing workplace relationships, particularly previously unhealthy relationships, requires changes in thinking, attitudes and behaviors on everyone's part. It's a process that can be very threatening to people's idea of who they are and what they stand for. In short, making the transition takes courage.

Summary

Seeing the Big Picture means keeping people's eyes on the horizon, letting people know what's ahead, and provide a compelling reason to go there. Doing so requires a *Leadership Coalition* who create a compelling case for change, communicate effectively, overcome obstacles and roadblocks, create a sense of real progress, and help make the Responsibility Culture stick. To assess often you engage in the five actions of an Emergent Leader, complete *The Emergent Leader Self-Assessment* found on the following pages.

THE EMERGENT LEADER SELF-ASSESSMENT

▨ Emergent Leader Actions

✔ Coach

✔ Offer Counsel

✔ Connect People to Resources

✔ Encourage Stewardship

✔ See the Big Picture

The Emergent Leader Self Assessment is designed to help you to first assess, and then periodically measure, your progress on increasing the frequency of Emergent Leader actions. The first time you take the self-assessment, you will establish a benchmark against which you can gauge your progress. Repeat the self-assessment as often as you like. The self-assessment is for your personal use; you need not share your results with anyone. However, you might want to ask one or more trusted colleagues to evaluate your progress by either reviewing your self-assessment, or by filling out the assessment on you and then comparing the results.

Identifying the Frequency of Your Emergent Leader Actions

Instructions: After reading each numbered statement, mark the number that most closely indicates your level of agreement with each of the statements which describe the five actions of an Emergent Leader. Mark the number that most accurately reflects your level of agreement with each description. In order make your responses more accurate, don't over-think your answers; rather, quickly mark your choices. After completing each section, total your score at the bottom of the page. Post your score for each section at the end of the self-assessment on the page titled *Plotting Your Emergent Leader Scores*. Review your answers and decide which *Emergent Leader Actions* you want to work on in the coming months.

SCORING

---

1 = Strongly Disagree   2 = Moderately Disagree
3 = Neither Agree nor Disagree   4 = Moderately Agree
5 = Strongly Agree

EXAMPLE

1	2	3	4	5	1 = Strongly Disagree 2 = Moderately Disagree 3 = Neither Agree nor Disagree 4 = Moderately Agree 5 = Strongly Agree
				X	I encourage my coworkers to take ownership for their jobs, deciding what to do, and how and when to do it.
			X		I encourage my coworkers to negotiate with each other to determine who is responsible and accountable for each important task in the group.
			X		I encourage my coworkers to share ownership for designing the systems, for removing waste and for improving work flow.
		X			I encourage my coworkers to ask our customers what they want and need, and to take ownership for delivering it.
	X				I encourage my coworkers to take ownership for their jobs, deciding what to do, and how and when to do it.
0	2	3	8	5	*Multiply the number of responses in each column by the score at the top of the column. Then, record your score in the space provided in this row.*
TOTAL = 18					*Record your total score for this issue in this row.*

Score Your Level of Agreement with the Following Statements About Your Emergent Leader Actions

					COACHING
1	**2**	**3**	**4**	**5**	**1 = Strongly Disagree 2 = Moderately Disagree** **3 = Neither Agree nor Disagree** **4 = Moderately Agree 5 = Strongly Agree**
					I consider it an important part of my job to encourage my coworkers to learn and grow.
					I make it a priority to share my knowledge and skills with my coworkers as often as asked.
					I give my coworkers opportunities to apply the skills and knowledge I've shared with them, so they can gain experience and confidence.
					I encourage my coworkers to apply the skills I've shared with them so that they can perform these new tasks without my help.
					When my coworkers are encountering challenges learning a new skill, I allow them to find their own solutions without interfering, until they ask for my help.
					Multiply the number of responses in each column by the score at the top of the column. Then, record your score in the space provided in this row.
TOTAL =					*Record your total score for this issue in this row.*

					OFFERING COUNSEL
1	**2**	**3**	**4**	**5**	1 = Strongly Disagree 2 = Moderately Disagree 3 = Neither Agree nor Disagree 4 = Moderately Agree 5 = Strongly Agree
					When offering counsel, I neither take ownership of problems and issues away from my coworkers, nor do I allow my coworkers to dump their problems on me.
					When coworkers ask for my counsel, I avoid offering solutions to their problems and issues; rather, I help them find their own answers.
					When counseling coworkers, I often restate what I've heard in order to help them clarify their thinking and to help them accurately assess their issues.
					When offering counsel, I encourage my coworkers to explore their beliefs and attitudes that may be contributing to their problems.
					When offering counsel, I encourage my coworkers to consider how their need to be right might be affecting their progress toward a solution.
					Multiply the number of responses in each column by the score at the top of the column. Then, record your score in the space provided in this row.
TOTAL =					*Record your total score for this issue in this row.*

					CONNECTING PEOPLE TO RESOURCES
1	2	3	4	5	1 = Strongly Disagree 2 = Moderately Disagree 3 = Neither Agree nor Disagree 4 = Moderately Agree 5 = Strongly Agree
					I consider it part of my job to help my coworkers find the time they need to get the job done.
					I consider it part of my job to help my coworkers build a business case to secure funding for additional operating expenses and capital expenditures.
					I consider it part of my job to help my coworkers get the help they need for an especially heavy workload, a pressing deadline or a special project.
					I consider it part of my job to help my coworkers secure access to any and all information they need.
					I consider it part of my job to make sure my coworkers and I have the authority and autonomy to take responsibility for securing resources.
					Multiply the number of responses in each column by the score at the top of the column. Then, record your score in the space provided in this row.
TOTAL =					*Record your total score for this issue in this row.*

ENCOURAGING STEWARDSHIP					
1	**2**	**3**	**4**	**5**	**1 = Strongly Disagree 2 = Moderately Disagree** **3 = Neither Agree nor Disagree** **4 = Moderately Agree 5 = Strongly Agree**
					I encourage my coworkers to take ownership for their jobs, deciding what to do, and how and when to do it.
					I encourage my coworkers to negotiate with each other to determine who is responsible and accountable for each important task in the group.
					I encourage my coworkers to share ownership for designing the systems, for removing waste and for improving work flow.
					I encourage my coworkers to ask our customers what they want and need, and to take ownership for delivering it.
					I encourage my coworkers to determine what needs to be measured, to design the measures, and do the measuring.
					Multiply the number of responses in each column by the score at the top of the column. Then, record your score in the space provided in this row.
TOTAL =					*Record your total score for this issue in this row.*

					HELPING OTHERS SEE THE BIG PICTURE
1	**2**	**3**	**4**	**5**	**1 = Strongly Disagree 2 = Moderately Disagree** **3 = Neither Agree nor Disagree** **4 = Moderately Agree 5 = Strongly Agree**
					An important part of my job is creating a compelling case for change when change is what's needed.
					An important part of my job is creating a sense of real progress when we're confronting tough challenges.
					An important part of my job is supporting a *Responsibility Culture*, where every person is responsible and accountable for his or her job and for the systems.
					An important part of my job is helping my group overcome roadblocks to a *Responsibility Culture*.
					An important part of my job is for me and my coworkers to help make the Responsibility Culture stick, even through challenging times.
					Multiply the number of responses in each column by the score at the top of the column. Then, record your score in the space provided in this row.
TOTAL =					*Record your total score for this issue in this row.*

Plotting Your Emergent Leader Action Frequency Scores

FREQUENCY OF EMERGENT LEADER ACTIONS	Plot your scores on the chart below marking your scores with an X. Then, connect the Xs, creating an Emergent Leadership Action Frequency Profile.					
VERY HIGH Frequency of Emergent Leader Action	25					
	24					
	23					
	22					
HIGH Frequency of Emergent Leader Action	21					
	20					
	19					
	18					
MODERATE Frequency of Emergent Leader Action	17					
	16					
	15					
	14					
LOW Frequency of Emergent Leader Action	13					
	12					
	11					
	10					
VERY LOW Frequency of Emergent Leader Action	9					
	8					
	7					
	6					
	5					
Emergent Leader Actions		Coaching	Offering Counsel	Connecting People to Resources	Encouraging Stewardship	Seeing the Big Picture

Steps I plan to take to strengthen my Emergent Leader Actions:

(1) Coaching:

(2) Offering Counsel:

(3) Connecting People to Resources:

(4) Encouraging Stewardship:

(5) Helping Others See the Big Picture:

Part III

TAKE RESPONSIBILITY
FOR DELIVERING CUSTOMER VALUE

Ralph Stayer, the third generation CEO of the successful family business, Johnsonville Foods, found himself worrying not just about the competition, but about what he perceived as "the gap between potential and performance." He observed, "Our people didn't seem to care. Every day I came to work and saw people so bored by their jobs that they made thoughtless, dumb mistakes. ... No one was deliberately wasting money, time, and materials; it was just that people took no responsibility for their work. They showed up in the morning, did halfheartedly what they were told to do, and then went home."

So, Stayer went to work to get to the bottom of the problem. After much soul searching, his first insight was that if there were problems, it was his fault, not the fault of his managers and workers. Then he set about trying to find a way to create an organization "where people took responsibility for their own work, for the product, for the company as a whole." Acting on instinct alone, he ordered change. "From now on," he announced to his management team, "you're all responsible for making your own decisions." As he described it, "I went from authoritarian control to authoritarian abdication," and the results were a disaster. "After more than two years of working with them, I finally had to replace all three top managers."

From his early failures he learned two important lessons. The first was, "I couldn't give responsibility. People had to expect it, want it, even demand it." The second lesson was realizing "I didn't control the performance of the people at Johnsonville, that as a manager I didn't really manage people. They managed themselves. I did manage the context. The power of any contextual factor lies in its ability to shape the way people think and what they expect. So I worked on two contextual areas: systems and structures."[33]

Authoritarianism has been the dominant organizational system and structure for centuries. Authoritarianism operates on the assumption that an elite class of individuals has the right to exercise power and control over others by virtue of accumulated wealth, superior intelligence, or position of authority. Paternalism, a close relative to authoritarianism, endows power to a patriarch or matriarch, who offers favors and protection in exchange for loyalty. Both authoritarianism and paternalism operate on the belief that pursuit of self-interest is a primary human motivator. Authoritarian and paternalistic leaders, perhaps because they are pursuing their own self-interest, expect to see the same motivation in the people around them. As a result, they create a politically charged environment where people gain power and prestige by helping their superiors solidify their power base. This means that there is a heavy price for most of the people who are not in power. As Patricia McLagan & Christo Nel, authors of *The Age of Participation* write, "In authoritarian systems, citizens, employees, and even customers are essentially subservient or—worse—disenfranchised and disempowered."[34]

In the twenty-first century, a number of powerful forces are changing the way business and governmental organizations think about leadership systems and structures. Whereas in the past, authoritarian and paternalistic systems controlled the dissemination of information, with the rapid growth of the Internet and multiple media outlets, information is much more widely available, making it far easier for people to make their own decisions and manage their own lives.

With intensifying global competition, guaranteed lifetime employment is becoming a thing of the past, and as a result workers are demanding more control over their work lives. Globalization has also blurred the boundaries between nations and within organizations, which has necessitated the creation of products and services that can easily flow across borders. Technology has significantly reduced the need for physical labor to produce products, and since individuals now have a much more significant impact on creating value for customers, workers' commitment and involvement is more critical than ever to the survival of a business.

Customers have gained much greater control over the marketplace. Before World War II, business leaders like Henry Ford could get away with saying, "You can have a Ford in any color you like as long as it's black."

Today customers have lots of choices. They can shop around. They can decide the kinds of products and services they would like. Put bluntly, organizations that encourage every employee to take responsibility for delivering customer value are surviving. Those that have not are not.

NINE
EXPECT EVERYONE TO DELIVER CUSTOMER VALUE

■ **IN THIS CHAPTER:**

Link Responsibility to Accountability
Encourage the Formation of *Self-Managing Teams*
Deliver Customer Value in *TransAction Zones*

Nathaniel Branden, Ph.D., the father of the self-esteem movement, describes "self-responsibility" this way: "The practice of self-responsibility begins with the recognition that I am ultimately responsible for my own existence; that no one else is here on earth to serve me, take care of me, or fill my needs."[35] Delivering customer value depends upon each member of the organization being self-responsible, recognizing that no one else in the organization exists to serve his or her needs; rather, he or she is responsible to the team, to the organization, and most importantly, to his or her customers. However, in order to consistently deliver customer value, responsibility must be linked to accountability.

Link Responsibility to Accountability

The terms responsibility and accountability are often used interchangeably. While these two words are strongly related, they have distinctly separate meanings in a Responsibility Culture. Let's define responsibility and accountability in this context, and then clarify how responsibility and accountability are linked.

Responsibilities
Tasks, duties, jobs, and activities belonging to an individual or group

Accountabilities
Results that an individual or group has agreed or promised to deliver to customers, colleagues, and the organization

Responsibility for individuals living and working in a Responsibility Culture begins with the freedom to make choices. Of course, choosing to take on any responsibility requires at least a minimum level of competence for the task. In self-managing teams, taking on responsibility also requires that individuals possess the skills to own their job without the need for supervision. Accountability to customers, to peers, and to the organization means that individuals working in self-managing teams are willing to deliver results, and when things go wrong, make it right.

The key differentiator between conventional hierarchical systems of accountability and accountability in Cultures of Responsibility is the link between responsibility and accountability. Under conventional top-down models, responsibility and accountability are purposely separated; that is, responsibilities are assigned or delegated downward (through the chain of command), but at the end of the day the person who delegated the task is accountable for the results (to a person of higher authority.) Persons in authority take the blame (although they often try to pass the blame along) for the problems and failures and are held accountable for them.

One of the unintended negative outcomes of this separation of responsibility and accountability is that inevitably a great deal of effort is expended on finding the person or persons who are accountable for problems and failures without looking, as Deming would advise, at the design of the system. This became evident when the American public asked how torture and prisoner abuse could have occurred at Abu Ghraib. A few low-level soldiers were tried and convicted for these atrocities. They were characterized as "bad apples" and "rogues" acting on their own. On closer examination of the truth reveals that these soldiers were operating in a toxic system that at the very least failed to discourage such outrageous behavior, or at the very worst, encouraged it. While these soldiers should be held accountable for their acts, it is more important that we challenge the operational philosophy that was responsible for creating such a toxic environment and hold the persons further up the chain-of-command who created it accountable as well.

In contrast, in a Responsibility Culture, responsibility and accountability are purposely linked. In other words, each person is responsible for the tasks they've chosen, and accountable for delivering results. If something goes wrong, the person who chose to take on the task is responsible for making things right. Shifting blame upward or downward is not an option. "The buck stops here" is the responsibility-taking mantra for everyone.

At Nordstrom, "Employees are instructed to always make a decision that favors the customer before the company. They are never criticized for doing too much for a customer; they are criticized for doing too little." One Nordstrom employee recalled a time when a customer who was shopping in her department realized that she had misplaced an earlier purchase of three bars of soap. "I went over to lingerie and got three more bars of soap and gave them to her. She thanked me and said, 'I can't believe you did this.' The bars of soap were only 90 cents apiece, but they produced a happy customer."[36]

The transformation to a Responsibility Culture at Harley-Davidson provides another example of an organization that came to understand, for the first time, the power of creating effective partnerships by establishing self-managing teams. Emerging from a period where the company nearly failed in the 1970s, during the 1980s CEO Vaughn Beals launched a number of drastic changes, first reducing their workforce by 40% and cutting salaried employees' paychecks by 9%. When the company continued to falter, they finally instituted a number of management-employee partnership initiatives.

As Rich Teerlink, Vaughn Beals' successor put it, "We had to identify some sort of strategy that could carry everyone forward everyone meaning employees, customers, and all other stakeholders. We had to improve operations. And I felt strongly that we needed to change the way employees were being treated. They could no longer be privates, taking orders and operating within strict limits. We needed to continue to push, and push hard, to create a much more inclusive and collegial work atmosphere."[37]

So, under Beals' and then Teerlink's leadership, the management at Harley-Davidson partnered with their workers to craft a shared purpose of Harley's future. Workers were no longer to be treated as second-class citizens. They were encouraged to fully participate in systems design and even had the right to say no to proposed changes. To pull this off, they had to establish absolute honesty between management and labor, systematically knocking down every barrier to quality they found. Management and labor partnered to design systems and structures that allowed them to be jointly accountable for delivering customer value and operational results.

By inviting workers on the front-lines of Harley-Davidson into the process of rethinking their systems, over time they were able to establish an effective partnership between labor and management that had not existed previously. Together, they created a system of responsibility that is the envy of industrial America today. People working on the production line have taken full ownership of every part of the operation from system design to quality controland the results have been amazing. By setting up self-managing teams, they were able to rise out of the red ink of the nineteen-eighties and become one of the most consistently profitable American manufacturers today, through good times and bad.

Like any company making the transition from conventional hierarchical management systems toward a Responsibility Culture, Harley's progress has not been without its challenges. In 2007 employees at Harley-Davidson's largest manufacturing plant in York, PA were on strike for two weeks before reaching an agreement with management on wages and health care benefits. This shows that even in organizations that have worked very hard at making the change to a Responsibility Culture, maintaining a healthy relationship between management and labor depends on maintaining a healthy social contract.

Encourage the Formation of *Self-Managing Teams*

In a Responsibility Culture, *self-managing teams* are responsible for designing systems capable of responding to the unique needs of their customers. People working together in self-managing teams fix workflow problems, increase or decrease production to match customer demand, and customize products and services specifically to meet the needs of each of their unique customers.

Members of self-managing teams take responsibility for every aspect of their operation. They design their own jobs, set their own work loads and schedules, and handle the finances, including setting budgets, planning capital expenditures, managing purchasing. They also are responsible for managing safety, maintenance and quality control, hiring and firing their own group members, and even deciding group member's compensation.

While serving as CEO of AES, Dennis Bakke encouraged the formation of Self-Managing Teams. In his book, *Joy at Work*, Bakke describes a visit he made in 1986 to an AES power plant in Houston. While there, he sat in with a group that was modifying the employee handbook. As the group tried to account for every possible contingency the handbook grew by several pages in less than an hour. Frustrated by what he saw, Bakke asked the group a series of hypothetical questions: "What if we eliminated it [the handbook] altogether? What if we did away with procedure manuals? What if we did away with detailed job descriptions? What if we didn't have an organization chart with boxes representing people and their jobs? What if we didn't have any shift supervisors? What if there were no written limits on what individuals could authorize the company to spend? What if all the specialist titles given to employees were eliminated? What if we created teams of people around areas of the plant to operate and maintain the facility, instead of letting bosses assign tasks and run the plant? What if each team could set its own hours of work? What if team members hired and fired their own colleagues? What if you could make important decisions rather than leave them to your supervisor or the plant manager?"

The initial reaction to his questions upset the supervisors. In fact, the next day they were threatening to quit. After he calmed them down he outlined his idea for what he called "Honeycomb," an idea inspired by his bee keeper uncle. Dennis explained that bees independently fly up to several miles from the hive collecting nectar before returning the hive. He used the analogy of a honeycomb to encourage workers at the Houston plant to "create an environment based on the same principles of trust, freedom, and individuals acting for the good of the larger team."

Two months later, he returned to the Houston plant and found that the workers had organized themselves into self-managing teams named after different types of bees ("for example, mud daubers, hornets, wasps, and yellow jackets.") These teams became responsible for "budgets, workload, safety, schedules, maintenance, compensation, capital expenditures, purchasing, quality control, hiring, and most other aspects of their work life."

In this radical new approach of allowing people on the front-lines to manage and operate AES plants, a new kind of work environment was called for, an environment where workers at every level were trusted to make decisions for the good of all the stakeholders. This included the owners, certainly, but also the workers, the community in which the plant operated, and the customers. In this bold new environment every worker was considered to be a "business person" who was responsible for maintaining resources (money, equipment, fuels) to meet the needs of all the stakeholders and of the community in which they operated. Since workers at every level were taking on so much responsibility and were becoming accountable to all stakeholders, Bakke insisted that these business people should "ask for as much advice as possible before making a decision to ensure the best balance of interests possible among all the affected groups, without compromising the ultimate purpose of the company to meet a need in society."[38]

Ricardo Semler, CEO of Semco, has taken on the challenge of establishing self-managing teams throughout his company for a very practical reason. As he observes, "If humans are organized in a huge, complex group, they need complex regulations and procedures to govern them. If their organization is simplified, the way they're managed can be simplified, too. Best of all, they can manage themselves. If you want to know what time each of forty thousand employees arrives in the morning, you'll need a complex system of time clocks, cameras, penalties, and rewards. If you organize employees into groups of ten people each following a customized seven-day weekend [Semler's term for the workweek is: a seven-day weekend], those clusters can be counted on to monitor themselves. ... At Semco, our units [self-managing teams] are always a size that permits people to know each other, understand the whole, and negate the need for excessive control. At any rate, we usually organize along the lines of a half dozen to ten people who directly interact."[39]

Nordstrom has become the perennial number one department store chain in the country by using self-managing teams to deliver outstanding service. Nordstrom employees are taught "The Nordstrom Way," which summarized briefly is "to provide outstanding customer service." Everyone in the organization understands that the specific products customers want can vary tremendously, while their expectation for outstanding customer service does not. To illustrate how well Nordstrom employees understand this point, here is a list of words and phrases a group of Nordstrom employees came up with when asked to think about customer service:

- Product Knowledge
- Courtesy
- Smiles
- Solution-Oriented
- Follow Through
- Coordination
- Professionalism
- Find a need and fill it.
- Don't make promises you can't keep
- Pleasing your customer[40]

Whether you shop at a Nordstrom store or work there, it doesn't take long to see that there is a reason that Nordstrom consistently out-sells its nearest competitors by a wide margin. The stores are organized into self-managing teams that focus on one thing: expecting every member of the organization to take responsibility for delivering extraordinary customer service.

Deliver Customer Value in *TransAction Zones*

Many organizations categorize customers by volume, profit margin or the type of product or service provided. For example, in the wholesaling business, customers are generally divided into three major customer types: "Customer Type A" for the highest volume customers, "Customer Type B" for mid-volume customers, and "Customer Type C" for low volume customers. Typically there are a small number of "A" customers accounting for a majority of their sales volume, so the wholesaler often allocates a small number of "A" customers to each sales team. Because there are typically a much larger number of "B" customers with moderate volume, the wholesaler will allocate more of these customers to each sales team. Finally, because the volume for "C" customers is so low, a large number of customers can be allocated to each sales team handling this category of customers.

TransAction Zones move beyond this simple form of classification by sales volume to design systems that can respond to high levels of customer variation. Rather than asking customers to deal with each internal function separately (sales, service, administration, warehousing, etc.) people within each of these functions work together to create TransAction Zones organized to serve the varying needs of their customers. TransAction Zones don't replace functional groups; they bring them together to serve customers. So, in a nut shell: *TransAction Zones are cross-functional teams that design systems and processes to give customers control of transactions.* In other words, people working together in TransAction Zones design systems that are able to respond to preferences, requests, and yes, even demands of each unique customer within a customer category.

People working in TransAction Zones do not assume that customers who share a set of common metrics (such as sales volume or customer demographics) want the same things. Rather, they assume that what customers want now and in the future will vary tremendously. They design systems in each TransAction Zone that are capable of responding to this variation in what their customers want. The primary goal of establishing TransAction Zones is to deliver customer value by looking at the business from the customer's point of view. They start the process of forming TransAction Zones by asking the following questions:

■ How can we make it easy for our customers to do business with us?

■ What is the best way for us to organize our TransAction Zones to convenience our customers, rather than merely convenience ourselves?

■ How do we ensure that every member of each TransAction Zone has both responsibility and accountability for improving the system, and for delivering customer value?

Typically, a wholesaler's functions include sales, delivery, merchandising, warehousing, administration, and fleet maintenance. The sales, delivery and merchandising functions are organized into small teams that call separately on a group of common customers. The warehousing group is divided into shifts. Administration and fleet maintenance operate as support functions to the rest of the system. While these functions must, to some degree, coordinate their efforts; for the most part, they operate independently of each other, trying to find the most efficient means of operation.

Organizing a wholesaler into TransAction Zones looks like this. Cross-functional teams are formed that include each of their internal functions. These teams meet regularly to discuss the unique needs of the customers they serve, how their needs and expectations are changing, and how the systems and processes need to be modified to better meet these changing needs. Since TransAction Zones exist to serve the needs of each unique customer, they may be permanent, meaning serving a long-term customer need, or they may be temporary, that is, serving a short-term customer need. Members of TransAction Zones design the systems and processes from the end of each process backward—the point where the customer receives the product or service—not from the beginning of the process forward as most organizations do. Again, TransAction Zones are designed so that customers drive the transactions, not the organization's policies and procedures. Customers decide what a quality transaction looks like, they choose the precise products they want, and they select the level of service and support they need.

Disney theme parks understand the TransAction Zone concept of allowing customers to drive the transaction very well. They do this by tapping into four elements of understanding their guests, what Disney terms as: "Guestology." Guestology focuses on: (1) NEEDS, (2) WANTS, (3) STEREOTYPES (expectations), and (4) EMOTIONS.[41] In other words, guests at a Disney park are there because they NEED a vacation, they WANT lasting memories, they have very specific STEREOTYPES (expectations) of how the cast members should look (Mickey, Goofy, Donald, etc.), and they want to feel the EMOTIONS of excitement and fun. For these reasons Disney designs their parks so that guests can easily choose the specific activities that fulfill exactly what they want from their experience.

Disney has set up each of their theme parks to be an inter-connected web of TransAction Zones. From the moment a guest passes through the ticket booth onto the grounds, the entire experience for their guests is designed to respond to their wants, needs, expectations, and emotions. From the layout of the park, to management of lines at each attraction, *cast members* (Disney's term for *all* park employees) do everything they can to make it easy for their guests to create their own memories. Every cast member takes responsibility for removing any roadblocks that may hinder their guests' experiences. Together they continue to innovate to find ways to improve the work-flow in the park so that they are delivering more of what their customers want.

When implemented across an entire organization TransAction Zones are scalable; that is, they can be formed at any time, for any customer, for any period of time. The number of TransAction Zones varies with the size of the organization, the types of products and services being provided, and the number of customer groups being served. Making TransAction Zones function well depends on encouraging every person working within each TransAction Zone to take responsibility for tasks normally reserved for managers and supervisors in a conventional organization.

Summary

Rather than depending on a manager or supervisor to delegate or assign responsibilities and to ensure accountability, in a Responsibility Culture accountability and responsibility are linked to every job. Individuals and teams are encouraged to form self-managing teams and cross-functional Transaction Zones that become responsible for delivering customer value.

TEN
EXPECT EVERYONE TO TAKE RESPONSIBILITY

■ **IN THIS CHAPTER:**

Experiment

Be Self-Directed

Be Creative

Set Priorities

Establish Policies

Plan

Remove TransAction Blocks

Complete TransActions

In conventional organizations managers spend most of their time "thinking," while front-line workers spend most of their time "doing." Thinking typically includes experimenting with changes to the organizational structure, the systems and processes. They also have the responsibility of directing the activity of those who report to them. Managers are the problem-solvers, using their creativity to find solution to issues, particularly those that aren't addressed by the organizations policies and procedures.

Managers set the priorities. They decide what work is important and in what order it should be performed. They set the policies both for what workers are expected to do and for how to deal with customers. Managers are also responsible for developing and implementing operational plans. This includes everything from annual budgets to introducing new products and services.

Managers bear the burden of creating, maintaining and improving the systems. It's their job to identify and fix problems that occur and to make sure that the people who report to them are completing daily customer transactions. Managers also measure the results of individuals and teams, often creating charts and graphs to let their direct-reports know whether they are hitting their targets and whether their activity meets the performance standards.

Contrast this with a Responsibility Culture, where the self-managing teams and TransAction Zones are the norm, all of these responsibilities are put in the hands of the people doing the work, the people on the frontlines, who are closest to the systems and processes and who are closest to the customer. Managers take on a supporting role, partnering with frontline workers and providing leadership as needed.

Experiment

People in a Responsibility Culture are encouraged to explore and experiment. Encouraging experimentation carries certain risks of course, not the least of which is *failure*. But as any scientist will tell you, today's failures are the price of future innovations. Even small incremental improvements cannot occur without a willingness to risk failure. In fact, failure is expected and even celebrated because people understand that each failure provides an opportunity to learn and is a step closer to success.

In order to make experimentation the norm, people must have the authority to make day-to-day decisions. They must be responsible for experimenting with the design and maintenance of the systems within which they work. In so doing, they become responsible for planning and executing *Nested Experiments* every day. Nested experiments, as you may recall, are proposed changes to the system structured as small experiments. They are designed to test the effect of modifications to systems and processes before making them permanent.

Nested experiments work like this: people observe the workflow looking for problems and failures. Next, they form a hypothesis (a theory of why the problem or failure has occurred and a possible solution) and design an experiment in which a small modification (a proposed solution) can be tested, including a precise estimate of the anticipated results. Then, the experiment is conducted and the results of the experiment precisely measured. The actual results are compared with the anticipated results. If there is a difference, however slight, they try to try to determine why the variance occurred.

Workers keep a careful log of nested experiments and their effects. The log lists problems observed, the countermeasures for each problem, the effect of the change, and the workers' reactions to the countermeasures. Staff members are expected to experiment as frequently as possible.

Be Self-Directed

People in a Responsibility Culture have the freedom to choose their own job responsibilities. This doesn't mean that people have the power to choose not to do unpleasant or difficult tasks. It means instead that they have accepted the responsibility for choosing to do these tasks and to be accountable for the results. It's the element of choice that is important. When people feel they are being coerced into doing unpleasant or difficult tasks, they are much more likely to either do the job poorly or not at all. On the other hand, when people are given the freedom to choose to take on difficult or unpleasant tasks they are much more likely to do their best.

Whether the tasks are effortless and fun, or challenging or distasteful, people should have the freedom to make decisions each day about what they will do and how they will do it. They should also have the freedom to design the systems within which they work, and be responsible for making improvements to workflow; they should have the freedom to do whatever is needed in order to satisfy their customers.

Senior leaders in a Responsibility Culture understand and have accepted the fact that no one knows the systems and customers better than the people closest to the work. Because of this it only makes sense to them that self-directed people should take on the responsibility for designing and improving the systems. The goal is to help every individual learn to become self-directed. Of course, this doesn't happen overnight. For individuals to become self-directed (empowered), they need to have mastered important skills, to be committed to their jobs and to have passion for their work.

As James A. Autry and Stephen Mitchell write, "real empowerment is not about taking power from the top and spreading it through the company. On the contrary, it is about you as a manager recognizing that your employees already have power. It is the power of their skills, their commitment to the job, and their passion for the work. This is not your power to give. Real power is power that you can recognize and honor by creating an environment in which the power can be expressed for the good of all. It is power *with* your people, not power *over* your people. In the same way, your own power comes not from your authority. It comes from your abilities, experience, and commitment. The real job of empowerment is bringing the power of your employees together with your own power in order to produce the best results for everyone."[42]

Be Creative

Creativity establishes a high level of engagement and commitment at all levels of an organization. Creativity goes well beyond the artistic: it means being imaginative, enthusiastic and energetic. This means that people have the freedom to work independently on projects they find interesting and challenging, the essential elements of intrinsic motivation. People design their jobs so that they have enough creativity to keep them engaged and committed to their work. When they become bored with or overwhelmed by their jobs, they take the initiative to swap responsibilities with their coworkers or to ask for help. As people experiment, they strive to be imaginative, inventive and original in their thinking. Each job includes elements of fun, energy and enthusiasm, which lead to a higher level of engagement with and commitment to their work and to their coworkers.

People in a Responsibility Culture must be encouraged to think "outside-the-box" and to try new things without needing to check for prior approval. This mode of thinking is critical in a culture where experimentation is encouraged. Rather than hearing phrases like "This is the way we do things here" or "We tried that once and it failed" or "Our policy says …" or "Our process dictates …," the members of self-managing teams are more likely to hear, "Let's give it a try and see what happens" or "That's an interesting idea, let's play with it for a while" or "I've never thought of doing things that way before. This could be interesting!"

One of the creative elements of TransAction Zones is that people working in them often come become creative in direct response to changes to market conditions or changes in customer demand. Well-established conventional organizations often don't see changes in market conditions coming. Their tendency is to either anticipate a continuation of the present conditions, or to be unrealistically optimistic about the organization's future. But market changes do occur often without warning. This is when creativity is particularly important. When markets change, the old way of doing things no longer applies; a new way of operating is required. Finding a new way of operating obviously requires creativity with people coming together to find innovative new solutions to the market change.

Another creative element of TransAction Zones is that membership is very fluid; people are able to move from one TransAction Zone to another depending upon how their skills, experience and creativity might contribute to the success of the group. In fact, often individuals are members of more than one team at the same time. They may even play different roles in each team, sharing leadership on one group or being more of a resource to another. This fluidity, sometimes called flow, encourages coworkers to find creative solutions and celebrate success together.

Creativity has a distinctively spiritual aspect to it, connecting us to the supernatural and to each other. In their book, *Leading with Soul*, Lee Bolman and Terrence Deal quote Harvey Cox, a leading American theologian at the Harvard Divinity School: "Man in his very essence is *homo festivus* and *homo fantasia*. Celebrating and imagining are integral parts of his humanity but western industrial man in the past few centuries has begun to lose his capacity for festivity and fantasy. The loss is personal, social, and religious. It deprives us of a central ingredient of our lives. It makes us provincial and maladaptive. It stills our sense of connection to the cosmos, of contributing to something larger than ourselves." Bolman and Deal go on to say that creativity is about *authorship*, "It's the feeling of putting your own signature on your work. It's the sheer joy of creating something of lasting value. The feeling of adding something special to the world."[43]

Set Priorities

Setting day-to-day priorities is dependent upon people knowing and understanding the direction and purpose of the organization. People in a Responsibility Culture know exactly what tasks for which they are responsible, and how what they do each day contributes to the success of the organization. In other words, they can see and understand how the results they produce each day contribute to the success of their own team and their organization. Seeing and understanding this connection is what enables them to choose priorities appropriately.

People working in a Responsibility Culture have fundamental business skills to understand financial and technical data so that they can determine their strategic and tactical priorities. Just as human beings require air and water to survive, organizations need two basic things to survive: (1) cash flow to fund current expenses and (2) profit to fund capital investments for the future. Therefore, in a Responsibility Culture, basic financial literacy (at the very least: read and understand a Profit & Loss Statement and a Balance Sheet) becomes a requirement for membership; all members know how to construct a budget proposal. Also, members understand and are able to use technical data unique to their disciplines (for example: anything that tracks workflow issues, causes of waste, and quality output.)

People working in TransAction Zones understand their customer's priorities and are able to respond appropriately. In fact, they understand that in order for the organization to survive, the organization's priorities must align with the customer's. While most organizations *claim* to be customer focused, few have developed systems for uncovering and responding to what customers really want.

Former New York City Mayor Rudy Giuliani recounts in his book, *Leadership,* how he helped the police department shift their focus in order to better set day-to-day priorities. He understood that the public is not interested in how many arrests are made each month or year; they are interested in making the city safer by reducing crime. "For years, the statistics in the Police Department that drew the most attention were the number of arrests and the reaction times to emergency calls. In fact, neither is the ultimate goal of a police force: public safety and reducing crime."[44]

By shifting the police department's focus from number of arrests and response time to 911 calls to reducing crime, our nation's largest city was able to significantly reduce the overall crime rate. How did they do it? To begin with, they rigorously tracked each type of crime in each borough from week to week. This enabled cops in each area of the city to determine how best to deploy their manpower and what policing strategies to use; in other words, to set their policing priorities that would directly reduce crime and make the city safer.

Establish Policies

In conventional hierarchical cultures, only boards of directors and senior executives have the authority to establish policies. Workers are expected to comply with the policies, not to challenge them. Policies are created to ensure that workers are doing what they should be doing, and to define for supervisors the specific performance issues they should be monitoring. Policies set by management also define for workers what they are and aren't allowed to do for customers.

However, in a Responsibility Culture, policies are divided into three categories: (1) *Purpose Policies*, what John and Miriam Carver call "Ends Policies"[45] set by the board, defining the reason the organization exists, (2) *Strategic Policies* set by the senior executive, defining the operating philosophy and a path toward the future, and (3) *Tactical Policies* set by each TransAction Zone defining how work is done and how customers are served.

Members of a Responsibility Culture understand, accept and support the board's *Purpose Policies* which explain the reason for the organization's existence and their expectations from the senior executive team. Everyone in the organization, not just the senior executive team, should know these purpose policies which are communicated in a variety of ways in speeches made by senior executives, in written communications, and most importantly in group discussions where members of the organization have an opportunity to ask clarifying questions.

The senior executive has the responsibility of clearly communicating his or her *Strategic Policies* which describe his or her operating philosophy, establish the boundaries within which business is to be conducted, and clearly define his or her expectations for the workforce. Members of self-managing teams and TransAction Zones have complete authority and responsibility for setting *Tactical Policies* that relate to the systems within which they work. They have this responsibility because they are the ones who must make the systems work; and they have the responsibility of challenging any policy that stands in the way of being responsible and accountable to customers. Setting Tactical Policies provides workers with the ability to control workflow, solve problems, and meet the unique needs of each customer.

Plan

In conventional top-down cultures, while people down the chain of command may be asked to give their input on plans, in most cases senior managers have already made up their minds. The process often works something like this: senior management ask for tactical plans generated at the "local" level by mid-level managers and perhaps even front-line work-ers. Often those at the lower levels learn quickly that they're simply "going through the motions" until senior management finally reveals their plans by demanding that the tactical plans conform to their pre-determined strategic objectives.

In stark contrast, Cultures of Responsibility expect people working together in self-managing teams to develop tactical plans and to help make them successful. Rather than relying on senior executives or power-ful senior staffers to develop tactical plans, members at every level of the organization are involved in planning and execution. Senior executives make their strategic goals known and then ask mid-level and front-line workers to develop plans to reach these goals. In the process, they ask for honest feedback on the workability of the strategic goals and are prepared to modify their strategic goals if necessary.

Members of self-managing teams are responsible for planning budgets, schedules, production, and delivery at the tactical level. They're also respon-sible for measuring results, and for modifying plans when results don't match expectations. They know that no matter how well constructed, plans depend upon a set of assumptions that may or may not turn out to be correct. In order for plans to be useful, they must provide for contin-gencies. Therefore, the rule on self-managing teams is: "Plan, but be pre-pared to modify the plan."

The U.S. Marine Corps has adopted a planning strategy that involves sol-diers of every rank. "The Marines don't distinguish between followers and potential leaders; they believe every member of the Corps must be able to lead."[46] In fact, when planning for battle, the Corps brings together a rep-resentative group of Marines from every rank, from private to colonel. Understanding the exigencies of war, they seek input from everyone gath-ered to draw up not one, but three battle plans. The assumption is that, in a flash of gunfire, a Marine of any rank may be called upon to step forward and lead, making battle field decisions about what plan to follow or whether, based on the circumstances, to come up with a new plan.[47]

Remove TransAction Blocks

People working together in a Responsibility Culture identify the causes of *TransAction Blocks* and for reducing or eliminating them. (TransAction

Blocks are anything that inhibits the customer transaction, disappoints the customer, slows the process, or causes other types of waste within the system.) Having the authority to remove TransAction Blocks has tremendous benefits for workers and even more benefits for the organization and for customers. For workers, TransAction Blocks tend to make life more difficult. Therefore, removing TransAction Blocks and improving workflow means getting rid of things that make work life hard to bear, such as overprocessing, waiting, excess motion, and any other kind of defect that may occur within the system which makes the job less pleasant and more likely to cause physical injury. Removing TransAction Blocks and improving workflow adds to the sense of empowerment for people on the front-lines and a gives them a greater sense of control over their daily lives.

Removing TransAction Blocks and improving workflow have obvious benefits for the organization, such as less waste and unnecessary cost, and of course deliver real benefits for customers in faster service and better products. Typically, says systems expert John Seddon, most of the calls coming into a telephone service center are the result of a company failing to do something correctly for a customer the first time. "In fact," says Seddon, "failure demand [runs] at a predictable 65% of [service center] call volume."[48]

Giving workers (including the service representatives) the authority to look into the causes of these failures and giving them the power to initiate corrective improvements to the workflow, dramatically decreases the number of failures. The result is better quality for customers (fewer failures) and lower costs for the company which can then be passed on to customers in the form of lower, more competitive prices and/or passed on to the bottom line in the form of higher profits.

Complete TransActions

Having the authority to complete TransActions, without handing them off helps people at every level of the organization develop a sense of ownership. People in a Responsibility Culture make every effort to complete TransActions, rather than handing them off to a coworker or supervisor. This approach gives the worker the ability to respond to special requests by customers and allows the transaction to be completed faster and with more customer value. By completing customer TransActions, members are responsible for delivering what customers expect—no more, no less. Much has been written in recent years about exceeding customer expectations—which seems like a good idea. However, experience has taught organizations that have tried to make exceeding customer expectations an operating principle, that while many customers may be delighted that they are getting more than they asked for, it turns out that some customers are not delighted; in fact they are unhappy that they didn't get exactly what they asked for. To those customers, too much of a good thing is not a good thing.

Even for those customers who are surprised and delighted the first or second time the organization exceeds their expectations, it is highly likely that at some time, the customer's expectations may begin to outpace the organization's ability to deliver, which means that even though you have delivered what you promised, you still have a disappointed customer. Therefore, it becomes everyone's responsibility to complete TransActions and deliver customer value in a way that your competition can't or won't.

James Belasco and Ralph Stayer, authors of the best-selling book *Flight of the Buffalo* write, "Maintaining long-term customers is about creating value—doing something customers want different or better than anybody else. Customers are where it all begins. Delighting them. Talking to them in their language. Selling them what they want. Learning from them what they need. Most of all, getting and keeping customers is about everyone in the organization owning the responsibility to get and keep customers. Every person, every day, views every activity, every procedure, every process, through the perspective of 'What is great performance for my customer?' Each and every person owns the responsibility for delighting customers. That's the right and only focus."[49] In other words, both the customer and the organization benefit when self-managing workers have the authority to complete TransActions in a way that delights customers.

Summary

Every individual and team is encouraged to engage in *Responsibility-Taking Actions*. These actions that are usually reserved for managers and supervisors in conventional environments become the responsibility of self-managing individuals and teams. To assess how much your organization encourages people to take responsibility, complete *The Responsibility Encouragement Assessment* found after Chapter 12.

ELEVEN
EXPECT EVERYONE TO UNDERSTAND AND IMPROVE YOUR SYSTEMS

▓ **IN THIS CHAPTER:**

Challenge Your Systems and Processes
Adopt *Systems Thinking*
Initiate *Task Force Projects*
Use the *Nested Experiment Model*
Apply *Systems Thinking Measurements*

Challenge Your Systems and Processes

It's been nearly 100 years since Frederick Taylor published *The Principles of Scientific Management*.[50] Taylor laid out a system which simplified jobs so that workers could easily be trained to perform tasks on an assembly line without having to think. It was the early days of the industrial revolution and businesses were just beginning to make the transition from an economy that had depended upon skilled craftsmen who built products one-at-a-time, to a bold new economic model where products were mass-produced.

Henry Ford, who applied Taylor's principles, dramatically improved productivity at the Ford plant by three to four times; and in so doing, reduced the cost of his Ford automobiles to an affordable level. Because of this incredible leap in productivity, Ford was able to dramatically raise the daily wage of his workers to a level where they could, for the first time, actually afford to purchase the automobiles they produced. Before that time, hand-crafted automobiles were accessible only to the very wealthy. There turned out to be a dark side of Taylorism for Ford's workers. Because it had become so easy to train replacements using Taylor's scientific management system, workers lived under the constant threat of being fired should they fail to meet their daily quotas. While worker's pay had substantially increased, their jobs had become sheer drudgery, their bosses had become bullies, and they had no control over their daily tasks. Using the principles of "Scientific Management" roles were established which separated the "thinking" reserved for senior executives and managers, from the "doing" assigned to labor.

Today most managers believe people working in the system, not the system itself, are the primary cause of errors and failures. While people working in the system, can quickly spot the problems, managers seldom see anything wrong with the systems they've created. When problems occur, managers are apt to conclude that the workers, not the systems they've created, have failed. Whether they intend to or not, managers use the system to bully employees into compliance. Even those employees who initially question the system eventually give in.

There are Systems Thinkers like W. Edwards Deming (considered by many to be the father of the modern quality movement) who have pointed out that people are not what causes failures in a system; to the contrary, the failures are caused by the design of the system. Deming proved that, rather than reducing failures, "fixes" imposed from the top frequently *increase* them. He pointed out that those at the top, because they don't work on the front lines where they can directly observe problems, cannot see the design flaws of the systems and thus, correct them. As a result, the systems they create are often wasteful, create barriers to quality, and are unresponsive to variation in customer demand.

A Responsibility Culture, however, makes the people who work within the systems, responsible for improving the systems, by continuously experimenting with improving workflow and removing waste. People on the front-lines working in the systems, who are able to directly observe problems are expected to take responsibility for correcting the flaws. Managers and supervisors take on the role of facilitators, teachers, coordinators and partners in the system improvement process.

In most organizations, the processes looks something like this: (1) an individual worker, a department, or other functional group receives an input (this could be an order, paperwork, a service, raw material, etc.), (2) a series of activities is performed (that theoretically add value) and, (3) an output is created (to another individual, department, or group within the organization or to a customer.)

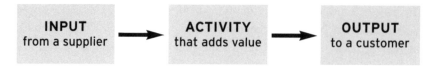

This process works fine, as long as there are no problems and as long as customers are willing to accept the products and services as offered. However, often problems do occur, and customers often want some kind of accommodation. The annoying thing about customers is that they want what they want, exactly the way they want it, which often is not what the process is designed to produce. Workers who try to respond to what customers want find that their hands are tied. In effect, employees who try to accommodate customers are forced to choose to either please their customer or please their boss.

Since mid-level managers in conventional organizations are the "keepers of the processes," employees are not allowed to address process problems, even when they are aware of problems and might have a solution. It places employees in a dilemma: if they challenge the process or try to work around obvious flaws they may be reprimanded, and if they stick to a way of doing business they know doesn't work they'll be unable to deliver a good result for their customers. Eventually they become frustrated and disengaged.

As former CEO of the energy giant, AES Dennis Bakke puts it, "We have made the workplace a frustrating and joyless place where people do what they're told and have few ways to participate in decisions or fully use their talents."[51] It's not that the managers who are keepers of the processes don't care about the people that labor within them or their customers. Of course they do. After all, without loyal customers and hard working energetic employees, no organization can stay in business. But rigid processes don't allow enough flexibility for people to take responsibility for responding to variations in what customers want and need.

In contrast, a *Responsibility Culture* views the organization's processes from the customer's point of view. They build flexibility into the processes by maximizing the ability of front-line workers to respond to the unique needs and desires of each individual customer. Since the keystone of a Responsibility Culture places the needs of customers in a central role, a new operational model is called for, in which people on the front-lines take the primary responsibility for delivering customer value by using *Systems Thinking*.

Adopt *Systems Thinking*

Systems Thinking is a framework that is based on the belief that the only way to fully understand why problems in any system persist is to understand the part in relation to the whole. Systems Thinking asserts that the conventional approach of focusing on solving individual problems without understanding how the design of the system causes or contributes to these problems often exacerbates them. This is based on the belief that the parts of a system will act differently when the system's relationships are removed and each part is viewed in isolation. Therefore, Systems Thinking studies the linkages and interactions between the elements that comprise the entirety of the system.

Systems Thinking views an organization's systems and processes from the customer's point of view. Viewing systems from the customer's point of view causes the system's designers to build flexibility into the systems and maximizes the ability of people working within the systems to respond to variations in customer demand. This is accomplished by following a disciplined approach: (1) study the system as it currently exists from end to end, (2) identify the variation that occurs, the severity and frequency of problems that exist, and the potential leverage points; i.e., places where a small change will effect a substantial improvement in the system itself, (3) plan and execute a series of nested experiments that will hopefully result in an improved structure of the system, and (4) after carefully measure the impact of the proposed changes to the system, and being assured that the proposed change will effect less waste and better responsiveness to variation in customer demand on the system, implement the change to improve the system.

Initiate *Task Force Projects*

Task Force Projects are a methodology for studying real-life organizational issues or series of issues that would benefit your work group, your organization and your customers. They are initiated to address a specific concern about a business issue. A *Task Force Project* is made up of a small team of people who meet at regular intervals (at least every other week for an hour or more) to work on improving workflow and removing TransAction Blocks. (Remember, TransAction Blocks are anything that inhibits the customer transaction, disappoints the customer, slows the process, or causes other types of waste within the system.) When the scope of the project is narrow, that is, within a department, a Task Force is drawn from members of the department. When the scope of the project is broad, that is, impacting multiple departments and/or customer groups, the membership of the Task Force is multi-disciplinary.

Using the *Nested Experiment Model,* members of the Task Force begin by *studying* the system from end to end. As they do so, they *identify* variation in the system, looking particularly for causes of failure demand. Then, they plan a series of Nested Experiments; and finally, they *do* the experiments and measure their results looking for reductions in variation and removal of waste from the system. Their measures are carefully designed to help them better understand how the system works and, most importantly, to deliver more customer value.

Use the *Nested Experiment Model*

The *Nested Experiment Model* is based on W. Edward Deming's famous process improvement model: Plan, Do, Check, Act (PDCA.) The Nested Experiment Model modifies Deming's PDCA model by following the Systems Thinking approach of studying the system from end to end, identifying the causes of variation, waste and failure, planning a series of nested experiments, and while doing the experiments measuring the results.

During the STUDY stage questions are asked, assumptions are made, a hypothesis is formed and data is gathered. In the IDENTIFY stage the variation of the system's output is documented and the causes of variation are identified and measured. In the PLAN stage nested experiments are planned and the anticipated improvements are predicted. In the DO stage the experiments are conducted, results are measured to see whether the proposed improvements have actually improved the system in a way that enables the system to deliver better customer value. Let's examine each stage, one at a time, beginning with the first stage: STUDY.

THE NESTED EXPERIMENT MODEL

Study ⟶ **Identify**

↑   ↓

Do ⟵ **Plan**

Study

The goal of the study phase is to understand why the system behaves as it does. This means that before beginning to gather data, a basic question needs to be asked: What is the purpose of the system? In other words: Can the system respond to *Value Demand*, that is, deliver what customers value? Once the system's purpose is understood and the organization is sure of what customers value, the system itself, i.e., the workflow, is examined from end to end looking for issues that cause *Failure Demand*; that is, demand on the system caused by failures in the system. Failure demand occurs whenever the system fails to get things right the first time. Failure demand is the primary cause of *waste* in any system.

CAUSES OF FAILURE DEMAND:

(1) *Over-Production:* producing products for which there are no existing orders or services or that customers don't want; creating waste by producing excess inventory and requires additional staff.

(2) *Carrying Excess Inventory:* carrying products that become obsolete as they remain in inventory; creating waste by hiding overproduction which may eventually lead to having to discard obsolete inventory.

(3) *Over-Processing:* taking steps that do not add value overcomplicates the process or builds in defects; creating waste by adding cost due to excess steps and time, over-inspecting, over-handling, requiring repair and rework, and adding to the bureaucracy.

(4) *Waiting:* standing or sitting around, waiting for the next step in the process; creating waste by adding to process time, lowering worker productivity, underutilizing equipment, creating bottlenecks and overstaffing.

(5) *Physically Separating Staff:* physical distance between staff members; creating waste by making it more difficult for members to communicate and to exchange information.

(6) *Untapped Frontline Creativity:* ignoring the creative ideas of workers; creating waste by underutilizing workers' skills, missing opportunities for experimentation and improvement, and squandering learning opportunities.

(7) *Excess Motion:* ergonomic issues—that is, excess twisting, turning, leaning, bending, and walking long distances looking for parts, tools, etc., and creating waste by wasting time and causing injuries.

(8) *Defects:* products or services produced incorrectly that are of no value to customers; creating waste by requiring the product or service to be repaired or discarded. Customers are forced to wait and inventories of existing products may need to be inspected for defects.

Suppose, for example, that an organization's purpose is to provide installation and repair services for cable company customers. The cable company's purpose is to provide high quality installations without the need for return visits, and to provide repairs as quickly as possible, done right the first time. As data is gathered about how well the system is working, the system's output is charted noting problems that occur (*Failure Demand.*) Based on the data gathered, one or more hypotheses are formulated about why the problems are occurring.

Identify

By studying the work flow from end to end and noting the level of variation in the system's output, causes of waste in the system are identified and the system's ability to respond to variations in what customers want is determined. Because customers don't all want the same things, it is important to know the variation in demand for each product and/or service offered. In other words, workers in the system need to be able to predict, with some degree of accuracy, the range of demand for each of its products and services.

Knowing the predicable range allows workers to design an improved system that can better respond to what customers want. After all, no organization wants to be turning away customers because the system can't handle the demand, and no organization can afford to bear the cost of maintaining a system designed for much higher customer demand.

Let's look at the cable company example again. The cable company might offer several kinds of cable services: (1) basic cable with no cable box or internet services, (2) full cable services with cable box, (3) full internet services with cable modem, (4) full cable and full internet services, and (5) full cable, full internet and telephone services, etc. An accurate measure of value demand would measure and be able to accurately predict the demand for each type of cable service installation and allow the company to build a system that is capable of delivering them.

Plan

Having identified what their customers want, the causes of each problem, and the frequency and severity of each problem, workers choose the most likely leverage points that might have the greatest potential impact on improving the system. It's time to plan a series of *Nested Experiments*. The goal is to make improvements that will enable the system to deliver exactly what customers want with less waste.

Looking at another industry as an example: Suppose the customer contact center at a life insurance company receives a phone call from a policyholder who has reached retirement age. He wants to know the current cash value of his annuity, his payment options, and the date on which he can begin receiving annuity payments. He also wants to know about the possibility of transferring the annuity to his grandkids and the tax impact of making the transfer, both on him and his grandkids. Further, he wants to know if his grandkids can use the proceeds of the annuity to help fund their college education.

Unfortunately, the insurance company has staffed its contact center with individuals who, while they have access to basic information on policies (available on a computer database), are not qualified to answer the kinds of questions the policyholder is asking. Neither is the contact center system designed to transfer the call to a person qualified to answer the question. The contact center staff person offers to have an agent contact the policyholder within three business days and provides a phone number to call if after being contacted by the agent, he has any further questions.

Understandably, the policyholder is unhappy with the transaction. In fact, he is so unhappy that he hangs up, calls the insurance company again and asks for the complaints department. Upon reaching the complaints department, the staff member handling the complaint once again explains that his company's process calls for a licensed agent in his local area to contact him by phone within three business days. Three days later, the local agent calls to say he would prefer not to answer the policy-holder's questions over the phone. Instead, the agent asks the policyholder to come in for an appointment at his office in a neighboring city (ninety minutes away) where he will be able to answer all the policyholder's questions.

Obviously, the insurance company's contact center system is not designed with the customer's perspective. As a result, the system's capacity to respond appropriately to the customer's request for information (Value Demand) is woefully inadequate from the customer's point of view, and highly wasteful and inefficient for the insurance company.

CONSIDER THESE QUESTIONS DURING THE PLANNING STAGE:

(1) How well does the system respond to changes in what customers want?

(2) Are there steps in the system that can be removed that cause waste or don't add value?

(3) What measures should be used to determine the success of nested experiments?

Do

The experiments are designed. Now it's time to complete the experiments and assess the results. During the Nested Experiments, measurements are taken that will tell whether they've successfully removed waste and improved the system's ability to deliver more customer value. As each experiment is conducted, the results are carefully monitored to determine whether the experiments have successfully improved the system.

As far as the insurance company example, the insurance company would begin by looking at the process from the customer's point of view, experimenting with redesigning the customer-initiated contact process. Clearly customers with questions want answers. So how might the insurance company design a system that is capable of responding to a wide variety of customer questions? They might start tracking not just the number of questions and complaints, but the nature of each question and complaint so that they can design a delivery system capable of responding to a broad range of calls. They might also experiment with staffing the contact center with more highly trained persons capable of handling and resolving the majority of calls. There are a number of system solutions with which they might experiment before finding a system that delivers more of what their customers want with fewer failures.

Apply *Systems Thinking Measurements*

John Seddon, a leading contemporary systems thinker describes customers this way, "Customers make customer-shaped demands; if the systems cannot absorb this variety, costs will rise."[52] What Seddon is saying is that this customer-adaptive capability must be designed into the systems. This is accomplished by asking the people who work within the system every day, not managers or supervisors, to become responsible for designing the systems, monitoring quality, and continually improving the system's ability to respond to what customers need and want using Systems Thinking. Systems Thinking recognizes the relationship between *Purpose* (what the organization does), *Measures* (knowing how well the organization is doing) and *Method* (exactly how the organization does it.) As Seddon describes it, "When one learns to take a systems view, one can see the waste caused by the current organizational design, the opportunities for improvement and the means to realize them. Taking a systems view always provides a compelling case for change, and it leads managers to see the value of designing and managing work in a different way. The systems approach is to design against customer demand,"[53] (the things customers want to see from you).

Systems Thinking applies three measurement criteria: (1) Measure only those things that relate to what customers value, (2) Design measure that help workers understand the system and improve your ability to deliver customer value, and (3) make sure that the people responsible for doing the work are doing the measuring.

SYSTEMS THINKING MEASUREMENT CRITERIA

What: Measure only those things that relate to what customers value.

How: Design measures that help workers understand and improve the system's ability to deliver customer value.

Who: Make sure that the people responsible for doing the work are doing the measuring.

Summary

Systems Thinking continually seeks to make improvements to the systems for the benefit of customers. *Task Force Projects* use the *Nested Experiment Model,* to improve workflow and remove TransAction Blocks: First, they STUDY the system they hope to improve, then they IDENTIFY workflow issues and causes of waste, then they PLAN a series of Nested Experiments looking for ways to reduce failure demand and increase the system's ability to deliver value demand, and finally they DO the experiments and measure their results to determine whether improvements actually occurred. Systems Thinking insists that you measure only those things that relate to what customers value, design measures that help them understand and improve the system's ability to deliver customer value, and do the measuring themselves.

TWELVE
UNDERSTAND WHY CONVENTIONAL MANAGEMENT THINKING FAILS TO DELIVER CUSTOMER VALUE

■ **IN THIS CHAPTER:**
Why Imposing Performance Standards Drives Away Customers
Why Setting Targets Causes Unintended Negative Consequences
Why Maximizing Output Creates Waste

Conventional management thinking utilizes one or more of three strategies intended to improve operational results: (1) Impose Performance Standards, (2) Set Targets, and (3) Maximize Output.

(1) *Impose Performance Standards:* The goal is to identify the specific actions and behaviors expected of people working within the system.

(2) *Set Targets:* The goal is to define the expected outcomes of individuals and groups working within the system.

(3) *Maximize Output:* The goal is to achieve maximum efficiency by maximizing the output of the system, and thereby reducing the cost-per-unit of a product or service.

What's wrong with imposing performance standards, setting targets and maximizing output? Unfortunately, these three strategies drive away customers, cause unintended negative consequences, and create waste. Before we examine why these three strategies fail to deliver customer values let's look at how they came into common use.

In 1945 Peter Drucker penned *Concept of the Corporation.*[54] His famous theory, "Management by Objectives" popularized the use of mutually agreed-upon targets and performance standards as a means of boosting operational performance. Unlike Taylor, Drucker spent little time observing and writing about work on the front lines. Instead, he focused his attention on management and management theory. While he wrote extensively about the "need for community" where the "knowledge worker's" social needs could be met, his organizational solutions were still fundamentally focused on how management could exert control over workers' activity and behavior, albeit more subtly than either Frederick Taylor or B. F. Skinner.

Influenced by Drucker's thinking, targets and performance standards, and production targets have become the norm in the past several decades. Performance standards and targets are intended to improve the level of performance in the organization by defining desired behaviors and actions. They tell workers exactly *how* to do their jobs. For example, workers might be required by their company's performance standards to produce products following a defined set of specifications. Similarly, distributors of a company's products might be required to follow performance standards for shelf-sets, displays, and point-of-sale materials.

Targets define the specific outcomes expected of individuals and groups. Targets tell individuals exactly how much they are required to produce in a given period of time. For example, workers might be given a target to reach a specific quota each hour, day, week or month; and if they fail to meet the quota they are at first reprimanded, and perhaps later fired. Distributors might be required to meet certain targets or quotas of product sold in order to retain distribution rights.

Distributors often make certain they hit their supplier's targets by maximizing their system's output. For example, they will, because it is demanded of them by their supplier, place a new product at every retail outlet in their territory. They know, in advance, from observing sales trends in each account that the some new product are highly unlikely to sell in certain accounts. Later, when those products remain unsold, they must be picked up by the distributor (if required to do so) and redistributed to accounts where the product is selling, or discarded. In industries where the retailer is stuck with product that won't sell, the retailer understandably becomes less inclined to do business with the distributor in the future.

The problem with performance standards, and targets is that they ignore three important facts that Deming taught and that other systems thinkers confirm: (1) customer demand is highly variable, (2) any system's outputs are also variable, and (3) since management designs the systems, workers have little control over how well the systems work and little or no responsibility for improving them. Therefore, achieving targets, quotas and performance standard is often not within the control of the people trying their best to adhere to them, and therefore, unintentionally encourages them to try to avoid responsibility and accountability.

From a motivational viewpoint, when people fail to hit a target, performance standard or quota, they tend to feel guilty, ashamed and responsible. Consequently targets, performance standards, and quotas often destroy worker motivation and morale and teach them "learned helplessness." When morale drops, the typical worker's energy is directed toward surviving rather than on improving individual performance or improving the performance of the organization. These are the very things targets, performance standards, and quotas are designed to enhance!

After CJ graduated from college with a degree in psychology, he faced the challenge that many recent college graduates confront, which is finding a job. The obvious choice with his academic credentials was to seek employment in the social services field. Instead he thought he might try his hand at jobs that might provide a higher level of income. CJ is a big young man. When I say big, picture one of those guys you see on TV in a "world's strongest man" competition. So, with his size and interest in physical training, he decided to get involved in the health club industry. At his first job interview, the recruiter extolled the earning opportunities to be had by working one's way into management. He was told that first he had to learn the business by selling gym memberships. CJ loved the idea of working in a gym where he could get regular workouts; and he was excited about the earning opportunity.

His first challenge was to memorize the company sales pitch. The sales track included the usual features and benefits of club membership, and also how to overcome objections. He was also required to memorize a series of corporate values statements. In point of fact, the company's values were an important reason CJ accepted the job offer. With his club manager's help he experienced some early success. But once he was on his own, CJ discovered just how difficult making a living as a salesman can be; and he struggled to reach his monthly sales quota. What disturbed him most was that his club manager encouraged him to do whatever it took to get prospective members to sign up, even if doing so clearly violated the company's stated values. To CJ, the company's values were in obvious conflict with a system that encouraged sales people to compromise their own company values in order to get the sale. Not wanting to violate the club's values and his own personal values, he left the organization.

CJ bounced around to different clubs trying to find an organization with integrity where he could be successful. Finally, he settled in at a club that felt right and where he could earn more than enough money to pay his bills. In less than a year he was named the club manager. The challenge he faced was trying to motivate his young salespeople to reach their individual monthly sales quotas so that his club could reach the sales quota set by the owner and so that he could earn his monthly manager's bonus. Upon becoming the club manager, he was happy that his club out-produced any of the other clubs in the company. Soon he found it a constant struggle to identify and hire young people who could survive in a quota-driven sales culture. Eventually, he had to leave the industry because he could not resolve his inner conflict between a sincere desire to serve his staff and the club members against the tyranny of doing whatever it took to meet the ownership's monthly sales quotas.

The main problem with quotas, targets and performance standards is that they are based on what the ownership or management hopes their organization will produce, usually an increase over the previous year. Of course, management can rarely anticipate changes in the economy or the market, which might impact customer demand; and they most often tend to ignore the variability of output caused by the design of the system itself. If the targets or quotas aren't reached, the blame is placed on the people working in the system. The conclusion is that the workers they've hired are not sufficiently motivated. One solution to the motivation problem frequently employed in conventional management systems is to turn up the pressure on workers; or simply replace workers who fail to produce. Of course, finding workers who can produce in a high-stakes environment is easier said than done. Another strategy to increase motivation is to find a tougher, more authoritarian manager or supervisor who is willing to push employees to work harder and longer. It's not surprising that in these high-stakes, target-driven cultures, workers and managers come and go frequently.

Why Imposing Performance Standards Drives Customers Away

Adopting performance standards, while intended to improve quality, actually forces customers to accept services and products as designed and produced—whether they want them that way or not. The problem is that customers don't always want things the way they've been designed or produced. Customers are notorious for wanting things *their way*. More importantly, performance standards impede the ability of workers to respond to variation in customer demand. In effect, workers are forced to choose between responding to a customer's request for a product or service that is outside of the performance standards (risking punishment), or conforming to the performance standard (risking alienation of the customer.)

Suppose a customer has purchased an MP3 player from a local retailer. The customer takes it home, opens the package, and begins reading the owner's manual. As he reads carefully, it becomes evident that the player he purchased has inadequate storage space for his music collection. He decides he wants to upgrade to a player with more memory, so he sets it aside until he has time to return to the store. Returning to the store eight days later, he approaches a customer service rep and explains why he would like to exchange the player. The service rep is conflicted. The performance standard states that he can make an exchange on products only when they are returned within seven days (unless approved by a store manager), and only if the seal on the original packaging is undisturbed (the packaging seal has been broken). Now the rep faces a dilemma. Because he is alone in the store and can't ask his manager for permission to make the exchange, he risks alienating the customer by sticking to the performance standard, or risks upsetting his manager by making the exchange. In most cases, the rep will stick to the performance standard and send the customer home unhappy.

Performance standards, no matter how well intended, tend to inhibit the ability of people working within the system to deliver products and services tailored to the needs of each customer. More often than not, an unhappy customer will simply choose to do business elsewhere in the future.

Why Setting Targets Causes Unintended Negative Consequences

Targets are a commonly used tool to define expected outcomes for individuals and groups. While people are working hard to reach their targets, they often ignore the unintended negative consequences. Let's look at the conventional management assumptions behind using targets, and why these assumptions are flawed.

> (1) **ASSUMPTION:** Targets motivate people.
>
> **RESPONSE:** Targets do motivate people; they motivate people to do anything to hit the target, including cheat!

In the mid-1990s, Shell Oil found they were under a great deal of pressure from the financial markets to provide greater shareholder value. An article published by Energy Intelligence Group, Inc. describes the situation.

> "The focus on targets ... became an obsession for staff whose pay was suddenly largely dependent upon reaching those objectives. When people's pay is half-dependent on very specific numerical targets, they start managing to their targets, and not working for the whole company."
>
> The targets served a double purpose. They not only provided a focus for employees. They were also a useful tool for communicating with investors, offering a simple way for the company to explain its business to the market, and an easy way for the market to benchmark Shell's performance. And with investors clamoring for ways to see if companies were indeed providing greater shareholder value, this was a tool that Shell and the rest of the oil industry were understandably keen to use."[55]

The problem is that while employees at Shell honestly worked hard to hit their targets and earn their bonuses, their reports became overly optimistic about growth in reserves (new oil and gas discovered) and production targets (petroleum products produced). In other words, under pressure to hit these targets, people at Shell resorted to telling management what they wanted to hear, even though actual growth in reserves and production remained flat. The people at Shell may not have intended to lie about reserves and production levels, but in the end, their "overly optimistic reports" proved to be untrue.

(2) **ASSUMPTION:** Targets set direction.

RESPONSE: Targets are not relevant in a Responsibility Culture because they are a poor substitute for understanding *purpose*. What is important is to ask these questions: "What's our purpose? How do we pursue our purpose? Are we accomplishing our purpose?"

To continue the Shell Oil example:

"There was a slogan saying 'if you can think it, you can do it'... It was just ink on paper, no substance behind it, style over content." Consultants also played a key role in LEAP—Leadership and Performance— a management development program that Shell set up in-house to run courses and training for its managers and to promote the stretch target culture."[56]

At a major business meeting in 1997 broadcast to Shell employees worldwide, executives wore "15% growth" T-shirts. Over the next few years as production failed to meet the targets, the targets were adjusted downward, until finally, with a new chairman in place in 2001, the targets were scrapped altogether. By then the damage was already done. Investors had been told that reserves and production capacity were growing when, in fact, they weren't.

Shell's real purpose is to provide energy to the world. Pursuing this purpose would include not only locating and developing new oil and gas fields, but also reducing waste and developing alternative energy sources as carbon-based fuels are depleted.

(3) **ASSUMPTION:** Targets give people something to shoot for.

RESPONSE: Can anyone know what's actually achievable? The thing to shoot for is creating customer value. Are there ways to deliver customer value with less waste?

Too often, as illustrated in the Shell Oil example, targets represent a something management hopes the organization can accomplish. The problem is that there are frequently a number of factors well outside the organization's control such as the economic, social or political environment, the weather, or even poor judgment. When Shell's executives set the target of increasing oil reserves by 15%, there were several factors that proved to be outside of their control. Two that leap to mind are: (1) declining world oil reserves, and (2) remaining reserves that were becoming more and more difficult and expensive to find and extract. While setting a target of 15%

growth was exciting for investors (Shell's stock price rose after the target was announced), reaching that 15% target proved to be beyond their control; production in the following years remained flat as Shell's reserves were not being replaced.

> (4) **ASSUMPTION:** Involving workers in setting targets will result in a better score.
>
> **RESPONSE:** Although this may indeed be true, hitting the targets may or may not do anything to create customer value, or to remove waste from the system.

Once again, the Shell Oil example shows us the fallacy of involving workers in setting targets in order to achieve a better score. Although workers at Shell participated in setting targets, they were, for the first time, competing with one another for funding of production projects. This competitive environment encouraged them to make projections that ultimately over-promised and under-delivered. While the short-term projection scores looked better, the long-term results didn't materialize and it actually damaged shareholder value rather than enhancing it.

Why Maximizing Output Creates Waste

The primary purpose of maximizing output is to bring the cost per unit down. Keeping the cost of production low is a perfectly reasonable goal. But the first problem with trying to continually maximize output is that this strategy ignores the fact that no matter how well a system is designed, the system's output always varies. Second, trying to force maximum output from a system in which output variability is already high actually increases the amount of waste produced by the system.

The conventional approach in manufacturing plants is to bring the cost-per-unit down by mass producing in batches. The problem is that since production rarely matches customer demand, this approach actually increases waste in the form of excess inventories which must be stored (waste) and perhaps sold later at a discount (waste), or worse, discarded due to obsolescence (waste). Also, while the plant is maximizing output of one product, it is unable to produce another product that customers may prefer, losing these sales to competitors (waste).

Anyone who has ever ordered business cards will understand this concept. Throughout my career, whenever I've ordered business cards, I've found it costs nearly as much to print 100 cards as it does to print 1,000. This is because most of the cost is in the "set up." Since I rarely use up my entire supply of cards before I need to update the graphics or make some other change, I find that over the years, I've thrown out thousands of outdated business cards and letterhead. Obviously, business cards are a relatively small expense and of little consequence financially. But imagine if you're mass-producing big-ticket items that become outdated or obsolete before you can sell them. What do you do then? You know the answer of course. You discount them, and if they still fail to sell, you give them away or throw them out.

There is a third and much more insidious problem with maximizing output—*the exponential growth of waste*. In the 1930s Alfred Sloan coined the phrase "management by the numbers." He posited that he could tell which of General Motors many divisions were making money using revenue and cost accounting. Following his lead, many organizations have imposed more and more sophisticated cost controls, spending enormous amounts of money on computers and software designed to track functions and activities. Unfortunately, this sense of cost control is an illusion and actually causes an exponential growth in waste. In truth, costs cannot be controlled by tracking function and activity. Rather, cost is reduced by removing waste from the system.

Removing waste begins by measuring the level of variation in the system's output. This can be done with a control chart that plots data points over time showing the highs and lows and averages. Charting the organization's hourly/daily/weekly/monthly outputs will reveal a great deal. But even more can be learned by charting time spent fixing problems. In a typical call center for example, upwards of forty percent of a service representative's time is spent on "failure demand," that is, customer calling to complain about a problem. Most organizations address this problem by hiring more call center employees and pushing them to maximize the number of problems solved per hour. Unfortunately, this "problem-resolution solution" only drives costs up while failing to address the real issue: doing the work right in the first place.

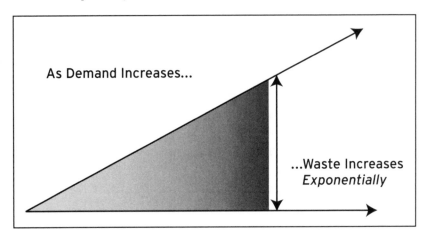

A company we were working with a few years ago was proudly giving us a tour their new "call-center" set up by the IT (Information Transfer) group to handle problems with their communication systems (telephones, computers, internet, intranet, etc.) They had added considerable call-center staff and created a monitoring system that featured flat-panel television screens that displayed the activity of everyone on the floor. They had established two targets: (1) respond to each phone call within two rings and (2) resolve each callers issue within five minutes. Sounds good right? Wrong. While the system worked okay as long as call volume was low, the wheels quickly came off the wagon when call volume rose (which happened often.)

What became apparent was that when the call volume was up, it was nearly impossible for the call-center staff to answer within the two-ring target; and because the problems were rarely solved in just five minutes, wait time for customers calling in grew longer and longer. To make matters worse, the call-center personnel had very rudimentary IT skills at best. This meant that they were frequently unable to solve a customer's problem without passing it along to a supervisor or a technician. Some call-center staff members would actually hang up on a customer rather than go over the five minute target! Here was another problem: the technicians resented receiving customer calls and were often either discourteous or wouldn't answer their phones at all, which meant the customer would end up on hold until they gave up.

Understandably, their customers were very unhappy, and the call-center staff members were helpless. The call-center employees were being pressured to hit their targets and were actually financially penalized when they failed to do so. Most of the staff simply gave up trying to help customers and simply stuck to the performance standard of reading directly from their customer-response scripts, which made customers even angrier. Because the call staff had limited knowledge and no power to make changes to the system that might actually prevent or resolve these issues, waste in the system continued to increase exponentially.

A Final Thought

Deciding to establish a *Responsibility Culture* by changing the social contract, encouraging Emergent Leaders and delivering customer value, can yield incredible improvements in operational results, in employee satisfaction and engagement, and particularly in the ability to deliver customer value. But make no mistake. Making this transformation requires a great deal of *courage* on the part of leaders to insist that every member of the organization be both responsible and accountable. And it takes a great deal of courage on the part of workers to give up their learned helplessness or bullying, and step up to be responsible and accountable. Breaking down the walls of old behaviors, obsolete management models, and ending adversarial relationships between management and labor is not easy. It takes an incredible amount of patience and persistence. The rewards—helping your organization succeed in a challenging world—are well worth the price.

THE RESPONSIBILITY ENCOURAGEMENT ASSESSMENT

■ Responsibility-Taking Actions

- ✔ Experiment
- ✔ Be Self-Directed
- ✔ Be Creative
- ✔ Set Priorities
- ✔ Establish Policies
- ✔ Plan
- ✔ Remove TransAction Blocks
- ✔ Complete TransActions

The purpose of *The Responsibility Encouragement Assessment* is to allow you to assess how well your organization encourages Responsibility-Taking and/or discourages Responsibility-Taking. Complete *The Responsibility Encouragement Assessment* and then use the scores to help you determine action steps your organization might take to encourage more Responsibility-Taking.

Is Your Organization Encouraging Responsibility-Taking?

Instructions: Read the description of each Responsibility-Taking Action. Then choose a score indicating how frequently you observe this action. Use the following scale:

0 = Never   1 = Seldom   2 = Sometimes   3 = Often   4 = Always

After you have chosen a score for each Responsibility-Taking Action you observe, multiply the number of responses in each column by the score at the top of the column. Next, record your score in the space provided at the bottom of each row. Then, add your score and record it in the space provided at the bottom of the box. Then, transfer your total scores for each responsibility-taking or responsibility-encouraging action to the page titled: *Plotting Your Organization's Responsibility Encouragement Scores.* Finally, write down the actions you'd like your organization to take in order to encourage more responsibility-taking.

EXAMPLE

0	1	2	3	4	0 = Never 1 = Seldom 2 = Sometimes 3 = Often 4 = Always
			X		Members of the organization have the authority to make day-to-day decisions about operations.
	X				Members of the organization are responsible for designing and maintaining the systems and doing the measuring.
X					Members of the organization establish their own priorities, processes and operating policies.
		X			Members of the organization choose their job responsibilities and are accountable for results.
0	1	2	3	0	*Multiply the number of responses in each column by the score at the top of the column. Then record your score in the space provided in this row.*
TOTAL = 6					*Record your total score for these actions here.*

Scoring the Level of Responsibility-Encouragement Actions Occurring in Your Organization

					EXPERIMENT		
0	**1**	**2**	**3**	**4**	**0 = Never 1 = Seldom 2 = Sometimes** **3 = Often 4 = Always**		
					Members of the organization are encouraged to explore and experiment.		
					Failure is expected and even celebrated, as members experiment with improving the systems.		
					Members of the organization have the authority to make day-to-day decisions when experimenting.		
					Members of the organization are responsible for experimenting with the design and maintenance of the systems.		
					Multiply the number of responses in each column by the score at the top of the column. Then record your score in the space provided in this row.		
TOTAL =					*Record your total score for these actions here.*		

					BE SELF-DIRECTED		
0	**1**	**2**	**3**	**4**	**0 = Never 1 = Seldom 2 = Sometimes** **3 = Often 4 = Always**		
					Members of the organization have the freedom to choose their job responsibilities.		
					Members of the organization have the freedom to make decisions each day about what they will do and how they do it.		
					Members of the organization have the freedom to design the systems in which they work, and are responsible for making improvements to workflow.		
					Members of the organization have the freedom to do whatever is needed to satisfy their customers.		
					Multiply the number of responses in each column by the score at the top of the column. Then record your score in the space provided in this row.		
TOTAL =					*Record your total score for these actions here.*		

BE CREATIVE					
0	1	2	3	4	0 = Never 1 = Seldom 2 = Sometimes 3 = Often 4 = Always
					Members of the organization have the freedom to work independently on projects they find interesting and challenging.
					Members are encouraged to "think outside the box" and are allowed the freedom to try new things.
					Teams are able to form quickly in response to changes in market conditions and customer demand.
					Membership in work teams is very fluid; people are able to move from one group to another to find creative solutions.
					Multiply the number of responses in each column by the score at the top of the column. Then record your score in the space provided in this row.
TOTAL =					*Record your total score for these actions here.*

SET PRIORITIES					
0	1	2	3	4	0 = Never 1 = Seldom 2 = Sometimes 3 = Often 4 = Always
					Members of the organization know exactly what tasks they are responsible for, and how their tasks contribute to the success of the organization.
					Members of the organization have the fundamental business skills needed to determine their priorities.
					Members of the organization understand the strategic priorities and are able to set their own tactical priorities.
					Members of the organization understand that in order for the organization to survive, the organization's priorities must align with the customer's priorities.
					Multiply the number of responses in each column by the score at the top of the column. Then record your score in the space provided in this row.
TOTAL =					*Record your total score for these actions here.*

					ESTABLISH POLICIES
0	**1**	**2**	**3**	**4**	**0 = Never 1 = Seldom 2 = Sometimes** **3 = Often 4 = Always**
					Members of the organization understand, accept and support purpose policies that describe the owner's or board's expectations.
					Members of the organization clearly understand the strategic policies that describe the senior executive's operating parameters and expectations.
					Members of the organization share in the responsibility of establishing tactical policies for operating their own work groups.
					Members of the organization are ready and willing to challenge any policy that stands in the way of delivering value to customers.
					Multiply the number of responses in each column by the score at the top of the column. Then record your score in the space provided in this row.
TOTAL =					*Record your total score for these actions here.*

					PLAN
0	**1**	**2**	**3**	**4**	**0 = Never 1 = Seldom 2 = Sometimes** **3 = Often 4 = Always**
					Members of the organization are responsible for helping to develop plans and for helping to make them successful.
					Members of the organization are responsible for planning budgets, schedules, production and delivery.
					Members of the organization are prepared to modify plans when conditions and/or assumptions change.
					Members of the organization are responsible for measuring results, and for modifying plans when results don't match expectations.
					Multiply the number of responses in each column by the score at the top of the column. Then record your score in the space provided in this row.
TOTAL =					*Record your total score for these actions here.*

REMOVE TRANSACTION BLOCKS					
0	**1**	**2**	**3**	**4**	**0 = Never 1 = Seldom 2 = Sometimes** **3 = Often 4 = Always**
					Members of the organization take responsibility for identifying the causes of TransAction Blocks and for reducing or eliminating them.
					Members think constantly about how well the systems are working and look for ways to improve workflow.
					Members of the organization don't hesitate to ask for help, if needed, to remove TransAction Blocks.
					Members of the organization understand they are accountable to customers and to the organization for removing TransAction Blocks.
					Multiply the number of responses in each column by the score at the top of the column. Then record your score in the space provided in this row.
TOTAL =					*Record your total score for these actions here.*

COMPLETE TRANSACTIONS					
0	**1**	**2**	**3**	**4**	**0 = Never 1 = Seldom 2 = Sometimes** **3 = Often 4 = Always**
					Members of the organization understand that they are responsible for completing TransActions without handing them off.
					Members of the organization are responsible for delivering what their customers expect–no more, no less.
					Members of the organization understand that they are accountable to their customers, to their group, and to their organization for completing TransActions.
					Members are responsible for measuring what they accomplish as they complete TransActions.
					Multiply the number of responses in each column by the score at the top of the column. Then record your score in the space provided in this row.
TOTAL =					*Record your total score for these actions here.*

Plotting Your Organization's Responsibility-Encouragement Scores

Level of Encouragement of Responsibility		Plot your scores on the chart below marking your scores with an X. Then, connect the Xs, creating a Responsibility-Encouragement Trend Line							
VERY HIGH Encouragement of Responsibility	16								
	15								
	14								
	13								
HIGH Encouragement of Responsibility	12								
	11								
	10								
	9								
LOW Encouragement of Responsibility	8								
	7								
	6								
	5								
VERY LOW Encouragement of Responsibility	4								
	3								
	2								
	1								
	0								
Responsibility-Taking Action		Experiment	Be Self-Directed	Be Creative	Set Priorities	Establish Policies	Plan	Remove TransAction Blocks	Complete Transactions

Increasing Your Organization's Encouragement of Responsibility-Taking Actions

Review your scores on the previous table and, based on your answers, identify the action steps your organization might take in order to encourage Responsibility-Taking.

(1) Experiment:

(2) Be Self Directed:

(3) Be Creative:

(4) Set Priorities:

(5) Establish Policies:

(6) Plan:

(7) Remove TransAction Blocks:

(8) Complete TransActions:

Endnotes

[1] A.D. Amar, Carsten Hentrich and Vlatka Hlupic, "To Be a Better Leader, Give Up Authority," *Harvard Business Review* (December 2009).

[2] Nathan Layne, Taiga Uranaka and Kevin Krolicki, "Inside Toyota's Epic Breakdown: Paying for a Screw-Up" (Reuters, Feb 10, 2010).

[3] Edwin H. Friedman, *A Failure of Nerve: Leadership in the Age of the Quick Fix* (The Edwin Friedman Trust, Church Publishing Inc., 1999, 2007).

[4] Carol S. Dweck, Ph.D., *Mindset: The New Psychology of Success* (New York: Random House, 2006).

[5] Philip Zimbardo, *The Lucifer Effect: Understanding How Good People Turn Evil* (New York: Random House, 2007).

[6] Russell W. Gough, *Character is Destiny: The Value of Personal Ethics in Everyday Life* (Prima Publishing, 1998).

[7] Max DePree, *Leadership is an Art* (New York: Dell Publishing, 1989).

[8] Robert J. Sternberg, *Successful Intelligence: How Practical and Creative Intelligence Determine Success in Life* (Plume Publishing, 1996).

[9] Rosamund Stone Zander and Benjamin Zander, *The Art of Possibility* (New York: Penguin Publishing Group, 2000).

[10] B. F. Skinner, *Science and Human Behavior* (New York: Macmillan Publishers, 1965).

[11] Edward L. Deci with Richard Flaste, *Why We Do What We Do: Understanding Self-Motivation* (New York: Penguin Books, 1995).

[12] John Seddon, *The Case Against ISO 9000* (Oak Tree Press, 2000).

[13] Alfie Kohn, *Punished by Rewards: The Trouble with Gold Stars, Incentive Plans, A's Praise, and Other Bribes* (New York: Houghton Mifflin Publishing Company, 1993).

[14] Daniel H. Pink, *Drive: The Surprising Truth About What Motivates Us* (New York: Riverhead Books, Penguin Group, 2009).

[15] Niccolo Machiavelli, *The Prince*, Second Edition (1469-1527), translated by Harvey C. Mansfield (Chicago: The University of Chicago Press, 1985, 1998).

[16] Inspired by "Eliminating Your Bad Spirit" from Phillip McGraw's book, *Relationship Rescue*, (New York: Hyperion Books, 2000) and Philip Zimbardo's definition of "learned helplessness" from his book, *The Lucifer Effect* (New York: Random House, 2007).

[17] Douglas Stone, Bruce Patton and Sheila Heen, *Difficult Conversations: How to Discuss What Matters Most* (New York: Viking Press, 1999).

[18] *Truth and Reconciliation Commission of South Africa Report*, released March 21, 2003.

[19] Philip Zimbardo, *The Lucifer Effect*.

[20] Ricardo Semler, *The Seven-Day Weekend: Changing the Way Work Works,* (Penguin Books Ltd, 2003).

[21] Tom Coens and Mary Jenkins, *Abolishing Performance Appraisals: Why They Backfire and What to Do Instead* (San Francisco: Berrett-Koehler Publishers, 2000).

[22] Jon R. Katzenbach and Douglas K. Smith, *The Wisdom of Teams: Creating the High-Performance Organization* Harper-Collins Books, 1993, 1999, 2003).

[23] Jeffrey K. Liker, *The Toyota Way: 14 Management Principles from the World's Greatest Manufacturer* (New York: McGraw-Hill, 2004).

[24] Dan Malachowski, "Wasted Time at Work Costing Companies Billions" (2005).

[25] Tom Peters, *The Leadership Alliance* (Video Publishing House, Inc., 1988).

[26] Bradford D. Smart, Ph.D., *Topgrading: How Leading Companies Win by Hiring, Coaching, and Keeping the Best People* (New York: Penguin Books, 2005).

[27] Robert Spector and Patrick D. McCarthy, *The Nordstrom Way: The Inside Story of America's #1 Customer Service Company* (New York: John Wiley & Sons, Inc., 1995).

[28] Peter Block, *Stewardship: Choosing Service over Self-Interest* (San Francisco: Berrett-Koehler, 1993).

[29] Ricardo Semler, *The Seven-Day Weekend.*

[30] Ricardo Semler, *The Seven-Day Weekend.*

[31] Ricardo Semler, *The Seven-Day Weekend.*

[32] Yvon Chouinard, *Let My People Go Surfing: The Education of a Reluctant Businessman* (New York, Penguin Books, 2005, 2006).

[33] Ralph Stayer, "How I Learned to Let My Workers Lead," *Harvard Business Review,* November-December 1990.

[34] Patricia McLagan & Christo Nel, *The Age of Participation—New Governance for the Workplace and the World* (San Francisco: Berrett-Koehler, 1995).

[35] Nathaniel Branden, Ph.D., *Taking Responsibility: Self-Reliance and the Accountable Life* (Fireside Books, 1996).

[36] Robert Spector and Patrick D. McCarthy, *The Nordstrom Way*

[37] Rich Teerlink, "Harley's Leadership U-Turn," *Harvard Business Review* (July-August 2000).

[38] Dennis Bakke, *Joy at Work.*

[39] Ricardo Semler, *The Seven-Day Weekend.*

[40] Robert Spector and Patrick D. McCarthy, *The Nordstrom Way*

[41] Disney Institute, *Be Our Guest: Perfecting the Art of Customer Service* (Disney Enterprises, Inc., 2001).

[42] James A. Autry and Stephen Mitchell, *Real Power: Business Lessons from the Tao Te Ching* (New York: Riverhead Books, 1998).

[43] Lee G. Bolman & Terrence E. Deal, *Leading with Soul* (San Francisco: Jossey-Bass Inc., 1995).

[44] Rudolph W. Giuliani, *Leadership* (New York: Miramax Books, 2002).

[45] John Carver and Miriam Mayhew Carver, *Reinventing Your Board: A Step-by-Step Guide to Implementing Policy Governance* (San Francisco: Jossey-Bass, John Wiley & Sons, Inc., 1997).

[46] Jon R. Katzenbach and Jason A. Santamaria, "Firing up the Front Line," *Harvard Business Review*, May–June 1999.

[47] Jon R. Katzenbach and Jason A. Santamaria, *The Wisdom of Teams*.

[48] John Seddon, *Freedom from Command & Control: A Better Way to Make the Work Work*, 2003 Vanguard Education Limited, 2003).

[49] James A. Belasco & Ralph C. Stayer, *Flight of the Buffalo* (New York: Warner Books, 1993).

[50] Frederick Taylor, *The Principles of Scientific Management* (New York: Harper & Brothers, 1911).

[51] Dennis Bakke, *Joy at Work: A Revolutionary Approach to Fun on the Job* (Seattle: PVG Publishers, 2005).

[52] John Seddon, *Freedom from Command & Control.*

[53] John Seddon, *Freedom from Command & Control.*

[54] Peter Drucker, *Concept of the Corporation* (Transaction Publishers, 1946, 1995).

[55] Energy Intelligence Group, Inc., "Exploring the Roots of Shell's Malaise," *International Petroleum Finance*, April 9, 2004.

[56] Energy Intelligence Group, Inc., "Exploring the Roots of Shell's Malaise."

Glossary

Accountabilities–results that an individual or group has agreed to or promised to deliver to customers, colleagues, and the organization (see also: *Responsibilities*)

Application Meetings–an opportunity for all members of the organization to gather together in small groups to talk about how the organization is progressing toward a Responsibility Culture

Bullying Behavior–any action used to control the behavior of others, such as verbally attacking, keeping score, finding fault, needing to be right, or refusing to forgive

Coach–the first of the five actions of an *Emergent Leader:* helping coworkers develop the knowledge and skills they need to do their jobs (see also: *Emergent Leaders*)

Connect People to Resources–the third of the five actions of an *Emergent Leader:* helping coworkers learn how to find and access additional resources they might need to meet new challenges (see also: *Emergent Leaders* and *Resources*) Resources include:

- INFORMATION: *made available to anyone in the organization who needs it; information is as transparent as possible without violating confidences*

- TIME: *found by removing waste, improving workflow, reordering priorities or negotiating with coworkers*

- MONEY: *making a business case for additional funds needed to complete a project or improve the system*

- MANPOWER: *making the case for adding people to a project, work group or system*

Customer Value–anything and everything that customers value and for which they are willing to pay a premium; creating customer values asks three primary questions:

(1) *What is the best way for us to organize to convenience our customers, rather than merely to convenience ourselves?*

(2) *How can we make it easy for our customers to do business with us?*

167

(3) *How do we ensure that our* Self-Managing Teams *and individual members have both responsibility and accountability for removing TransAction Blocks from the workflow and for delivering value to our customers?*

Deputy Fife Syndrome–asserting control or authority in an inappropriate or destructive manner as a bully

Emergent Leader–an individual who step forward to lead at the precise moment the team can benefit from his or her to lead skills and/or experience using one or more of the following leadership actions:

- ▪ Coach: *helping coworkers develop the knowledge and skills they need to do their jobs*

- ▪ Offer Counsel: *helping coworkers to learn how to solve everyday issues and problems*

- ▪ Connect People to Resources: *helping coworkers learn how to find and access the resources they might need to meet new challenges*

- ▪ Encourage Stewardship: *encouraging coworkers to take complete ownership for their jobs and of the systems*

- ▪ See the Big Picture: *helping everyone understand how each job supports the larger purpose of the organization*

The Emergent Leader Coaching Guidelines–

- ▪ Guidelines for Coaching:

  (1) *Look for a teachable moment before offering to coach.*

  (2) *Ask for permission before beginning to coach.*

  (3) *Offer coaching as a colleague, not as a superior.*

  (4) *Be willing to coach anyone who asks for help.*

- ▪ Guidelines for Being Coached:

  (1) *Ask for coaching whenever you need help.*

  (2) *Be open to coaching from anyone who offers to help without becoming defensive.*

  (3) *Listen to and act on coaching tips with a "growth mindset" (a willingness to learn.)*

  (4) *Give your coach feedback by asking clarifying questions.*

Encourage Stewardship–the fourth of the five actions of an Emergent Leader: creating an environment where workers are able to take complete ownership for their individual jobs and for the systems (see also: *Emergent Leader*)

Intrinsic Motivation–"being motivated by the reward of the activity itself" originally defined by psychologist Harry Harlow, PhD (1906–1981)

Leadership Coalition–Senior, mid-level and front-line leaders who, together, create a compelling case for change, communicate effectively, overcome obstacles and roadblocks, create a sense of real progress, and help make the Responsibility Culture stick.

Learned Helplessness–a syndrome of passivity, dependency, and depression brought on by a loss of personal identity when individuals are subjected to arbitrary continual control of their behavior; these behaviors include being passive-aggressive, creating diversions, playing the victim, avoiding, and giving up

More and Less Coaching Model:

■ RECOGNIZE A *TEACHABLE* MOMENT

■ EMPATHIZE WITH THE LEARNER

■ MAKE AN OFFER TO COACH

■ COACH
   I suggest more *of …*
   I suggest less *of …*

■ CHECK WITH THE LEARNER ON THE EFFECTIVENESS OF THE COACHING POINTS

Nested Experiments–proposed changes to the system structured as small experiments. They are designed to test the effect of modifications to systems and processes before making them permanent.

Nested Experiment Model:

■ STUDY: *study the system from end to end, looking for causes of variation*

■ IDENTIFY: *identify opportunities to remove waste and improve work-flow*

■ PLAN: *plan and execute a series of nested experiments*

■ DO: *measure the results of the nested experiments*

Offer Counsel–the second of the five actions of an Emergent Leader: helping coworkers to learn how to solve problems independently (see also: *Emergent Leader*)

Responsibilities–tasks, duties, jobs, and activities belonging to an individual or group (see also: *Accountability* and *Responsibility-Taking Actions*)

Responsibility-Taking Actions:

- EXPERIMENT: *conducting daily nested experiments intended to make incremental improvements in the systems within which one works*

- BE SELF-DIRECTED: *owning one's job without the need for supervision or external audits*

- BE CREATIVE: *using one's creativity, imagination, enthusiasm and energy to improve workflow, remove waste and deliver solutions*

- SET PRIORITIES: *having the authority to own one's day-to-day priorities*

- ESTABLISH POLICIES: *having the authority to establish tactical policies which define how work is done and how one's customers are served*

- PLAN: *having the authority and responsibility for making and modifying plans for one's own work*

- REMOVE TRANSACTION BLOCKS: *having the authority, responsibility and accountability for making meaningful changes and improvements to the systems and processes within which one works*

- COMPLETE TRANSACTIONS: *having the authority, responsibility and accountability for making TransActions and delivering solutions for customers*

See the Big Picture–the fifth of the five actions of an Emergent Leader: helping others in the organization see how what they are doing supports the larger purpose of the organization. By seeing the big picture, self-directed workers have the information they need to take full ownership of the systems within which they work and for delivering solutions for customers (see also: *Emergent Leader*)

Self-Managing Teams–teams of people who take responsibility for designing systems capable of responding to the unique needs of their customers. People working together in Self-Managing Teams fix workflow problems, increase or decrease production to match customer demand, and customize products and services specifically to meet the needs of each of their unique customers

Shared Values–(*LCI's Eight Shared Values™*)

- TRUTH: *Sharing the truth with everyone*

- TRUST: *Trusting one's coworkers and being trustworthy*

- MENTORING: *Being open to mentoring from anyone*

- RECEPTIVITY: *Being receptive to new ideas regardless of their source*

- RISK-TAKING: *Taking personal risk for the organization's sake*

■ GIVING CREDIT: *Recognizing the contributions of coworkers*

■ HONESTY: *Being honest and ethical in all matters*

■ SELFLESSNESS: *Putting the interests of others before one's own*

Systems Thinking–a framework that is based on the belief that the only way to fully understand why problems in any system persist is to understand the *part* in relation to the *whole*. Systems Thinking asserts that the conventional approach of focusing on solving individual problems without understanding how the design of the system causes or contributes to these problems often exacerbates them. This is based on the belief that the parts of a system will act differently when the system's relationships are removed and each part is viewed in isolation. In short, Systems Thinking studies the linkages and interactions between the elements that comprise the entirety of the system.

Systems Thinking Measurement Criteria:

■ WHAT: *Measure only those things that relate to what customers value*

■ HOW: *Design measures that help workers understand the system and improve your ability to deliver customer value*

■ WHO: *Make sure that the people responsible for doing the work are doing the measuring*

Task Force Projects–small teams of people use the *Nested Experiment Model* to improve workflow, remove TransAction Blocks and deliver better customer value

Teachable Moment–that moment when you're ready to be receptive to coaching and ready to hear and act on the information and direction a coach can provide

Three-Stage Counseling Model:

    I. INQUIRY STAGE
       (a) *Open-Ended Questions*
       (b) *Restating*

    II. COUNSELING STAGE
       (a) *Observations*
       (b) *Counseling*

    III. DEBRIEFING STAGE
       (a) *Next Steps*
       (b) *Counseling Feedback*

TransAction Blocks–anything that inhibits a transaction, disappoints the customer, slows the process, or causes other types of waste within the system; anything that impedes the organization's ability to respond to changes in what customers want

TransAction Zones–cross-functional teams in which customers take control of the transaction; they are organized to make it easy for customers to do business with the organization, and expect members of the TransAction Zone to take responsibility for removing TransAction Blocks and improving workflow.

Values & Attitude Study™–the most comprehensive measure of corporate cultures available in the world today. It measures values tension, motivation, and employee engagement; and compares the health of your organization's culture to organizations all over the world. The study has confirmed a strong correlation between the health of the organization's culture and operational results. Therefore, your organization's results are a strong predictor of your organization's future success.

Values Tension™–the interpersonal conflict that results when there is a gap between what people expect regarding the eight Shared Values and what they actually observe from their managers and coworkers

Acknowledgments

"Some luck lies in not getting what you thought you wanted but getting what you have, which once you have got it you may be smart enough to see is what you would have wanted had you known."
—GARRISON KEILLOR, creator and host of A PRAIRIE HOME COMPANION

I'm a lucky man. I didn't get what I thought I wanted when I began my career as a public school choir teacher—to be a world-class choral conductor at a major university. What I got instead has been a winding road of a career: first teaching in public schools, then becoming a Certified Financial Planner™, then doing corporate training for a Fortune 500 company, and for the last several years trying to sell the outrageous idea that in the right working environment, ordinary people can and will do the most extraordinary things for their organizations and for their customers.

So many people have influenced me along the way; not the least is my long-time friend, coauthor, and founder of LCI, Rob Lebow. Rob Lebow is truly one of the most passionate people I've ever met. His unswerving devotion to changing the world with Shared Values has been an inspiration to me. Most of the ideas presented in this book are not mine alone; many are Rob's creation. Others spring from the work of creative and talented authors and researchers; still others are the fruit of much thought and discussion between Rob and me, and, of course, some are my own creation. Over the last many years, we at LCI have tested these ideas with the help of our clients who share our passion for creating a Responsibility Culture.

I'd also like to thank the people who have significantly influenced my life, my thinking, and my personal growth: my parents and first mentors, LeRoy and Connie Spitzer, and my wife and best friend, Laurie Spitzer.

I'd also like to acknowledge the profound influence of the faith communities of which I have been a part throughout my life where I've encountered so many people who, in choosing to serve others, help create a *Responsibility Culture*.

My ideas have been highly influenced by a number of innovative thinkers. At the top of the list are four men: Dennis Bakke, co-founder of AES and founder of Imagine Schools (*Joy at Work*), Yvon Chouinard, founder and owner of Patagonia (*Let My People Go Surfing*), John Seddon, occupational psychologist and management thinker (*Freedom from Command & Control*), and Ricardo Semler, CEO of Brazil-based Semco (*The Seven-Day Weekend*).

Other writers whose ideas have influenced my thinking are *The Art of Possibility* by Rosamund Stone-Zander and Benjamin Zander; *Difficult Conversations* by Douglas Stone, Bruce Patton and Sheila Heen; *The Surprising Truth About What Motivates Us* by Daniel H. Pink; *A Failure of Nerve* by Ed Friedman; *Freedom and Accountability at Work* by Peter Kostenbaum and Peter Block; *A General Theory of Love* by Thomas Lewis, M.D., Fari Amini, M.D. and Richard Lannon, M.D.; *Intrinsic Motivation at Work* by Kenneth Thomas; *Leadership is an Art* by Max DePree; *Leading Change* by John Kotter; *Leading with Soul* by Lee Bolman and Terrence Deal; *The Lucifer Effect* by Philip Zimbardo, Ph.D.; *Mindset* by Carol Dweck, Ph.D.; Punished by Rewards by Alfie Kohn; *Real Power* by James Autry and Stephen Mitchell; *Relationship Rescue* by Phillip McGraw, Ph.D.; *Servant Leadership* by Robert Greenleaf; *Stewardship* by Peter Block; *Successful Intelligence* by Robert Sternberg; *Taking Responsibility* by Nathaniel Branden; *The Wisdom of Teams* by Jon Katzenbach and Douglas Smith; and *Why We Do What We Do* by Edward Deci, Ph.D.

—RANDY SPITZER

Note

This book supports existing curriculum marketed by *Responsibility Cultures* including: *Taking Responsibility Workshops, The Shared Values Guidelines, Task Force Projects, Self-Managing Teams and TransAction Zones, Accountability Agreements*, and *People Systems*. For more information or to subscribe to our monthly newsletter, *e-mergent Leader News*, visit *ResponsibilityCultures.com*.

Index

A

Abolishing Performance Appraisals
(Coens/Jenkins), 65
Accountabilities, 167
    definition, 113
    hierarchical systems, 113
Activity, direction, 31
Age of Participation, The (McLagan/Nel),
    110
Analytical intelligence, 13
Andy Griffith Show, The, 3
Application Meetings, 95–96, 167
Authoritarianism, organizational
    system/structure, 110
Authority, assertion (behavior), 4
Authorship, 126
Autonomy, motivation driver, 21
Autry, James A., 124–125
Avoidance, 41–42
    frequency, scoring, 51
    reduction, 54

B

Bakke, Dennis, 116, 134
Beals, Vaughn, 114–115
Belasco, James, 131
Big picture, understanding, 170
    emergent leader action, 105
        strengthening, 107
Big picture (understanding), emergent
    leader impact, 59, 91
Blame, shifting (avoidance), 114
Bolman, Lee, 126
Bosses
    allies, gaining, 27
    skill/knowledge, assumptions, 64
Branden, Nathaniel, 112
Bullies, social dynamics, 6
Bullying, overcoming, 23
Bullying behavior, 5–6, 167
    reduction, steps, 53

C

Change, creation, 92–93
Character
    choice, 11
    trust component, 11
Chouinard, Yvon, 91–92, 94
Coaches, 167
    Emergent Leaders, impact, 58, 60
Coaching
    assumptions, challenge, 63–67
    decision, 66

Emergent Leader action, 101
    strengthening, 107
    guidelines, 68
    model, usage, 61–63
Coens, Tom, 65
Command-and-control model, 80–81
Communication
    breakdown, 74
    trust component, 11
Compensation system, change, 38–39
Competency, trust component, 11
Competitors, negative characterization, 31
Complacency, dangers, 94–95
Concept of the Corporation (Drucker),
    143–144
Contact, avoidance, 43
Control, assertion (behavior), 4
Conversation, types, 26–27
Coping mechanisms, 24–25
Corporate malfeasance, 15–16
Corporate scorekeeping, 27–28
Correctness (rightness), necessity, 30–32
    frequency, scoring, 48
    reduction, 53
Cost-per-unit, reduction (manufacturing
    approach), 150
Counsel
    Emergent Leader action, 102
        strengthening, 107
    Emergent Leaders, impact, 58, 69
    offer, 71, 169
        Shared Values, usage, 72–73
    Three-Stage Counseling Model,
        usage, 69–72
Counseling
    feedback, 72
    stage (Three-Stage Counseling Model
        stage), 71
Coworkers
    allies, gaining, 27
    contributions, recognition, 76
    emergent leader response, 64
    honesty/ethics, 9, 15–16
    relationship, rebuilding, 43–44
    resources, discovery, 82
    tension, 40
    time, increase (discovery), 81
Cox, Harvey, 126
Creative intelligence, 13